This book belongs to:_____

If this book has wandered off... Finder, please contact Owner at:

_____

I, Teresa LeYung Ryan, say: "Whether you want to be your own publisher or sell rights to another publisher, attract readers now! Whether you write fiction, narrative non-fiction or prescriptive non-fiction ("how to" books, like this one), you are THE expert of your experiences and an authority in your field. Make your name synonymous with the themes/issues/subject matters in your book. Help your fans find you! Build your platform in 22 days. I cheer for you!"

WHY did I write *BUILD YOUR WRITER'S PLATFORM & FANBASE IN 22 DAYS: Attract Agents, Editors, Publishers, Readers, and Media Attention NOW* ?

- To help YOU thrive in today's publishing arena.

WHAT is a platform?
- Making your name stand for something—to attract targeted consumers who are likely to buy what you have to sell.

WHAT you'll need in order to fully benefit from this workbook:

- A name
- Something to sell – fiction or non-fiction literary project
- Basic computer skills (take a course; ask a friend to show you)
- Access to the Internet, a keyboard and mouse (libraries have them)
- An email address (sign up for a free address with Gmail, Yahoo, Hotmail, etc. if you don't already have one)
- Determination

Build your name, beat the game. You too can be happily published.

http://22DaysToBuildPlatform.com

ISBN-13: 978-0-9830100-0-5

I0027136

BUILD
YOUR WRITER'S PLATFORM
& FANBASE
IN 22 DAYS:
Attract Agents, Editors, Publishers, Readers, and Media Attention NOW

Writing Career Coach

Teresa LeYung Ryan

GraceArt Publishing
Oakland, California
http://GraceArtPublishing.com
http://22DaysToBuildPlatform.com

BUILD YOUR WRITER'S PLATFORM & FANBASE IN 22 DAYS contains secret keys. I am Writing Career Coach Teresa, the creator of this workbook/playbook. To honor me, yourself, and all the writers who have been, are, will be coached by me, please do not give away any part of this workbook/playbook. If you want to help friends, encourage them to attend my "Major League Tryouts to Build Your Platform" workshops or tell them to visit my websites/blogs. Cheers!

Table of Contents

Whether you're writing fiction, narrative non-fiction or prescriptive non-fiction . . . build your platform/name, stand out in a crowd! Create your fanbase and you'll attract agents, acquisition editors, publishers, more readers, and the media. Yes! You can build your platform *while* writing your book!

Where are you today?

You want to attract attention while you are <u>considering</u> publication routes:	• Looking for the right agent who will pitch your work to acquisition editors at publishing houses? • Pitching to acquisition editors at publishing houses yourself? • You are your own publisher?	You want to continue attracting attention <u>after</u> publication:

What is the game and WHO are the players?

The game is the fiercely competitive arena of the publishing world. The players (writing various genres in fiction and non-fiction) are:

- Authors with wonderful projects but have been turned down by publishers because they have no platform/fanbase.
- Authors with proven track record / platform / fan base / celebrity status.
- Authors who are also seasoned publishers or promoters.
- Authors with no budget, limited budgets, and big budgets.
- Authors who know a little bit about the publishing industry.
- Authors who are looking for agents to represent them.
- Authors who choose to publish their own work.
- Authors who have sold rights-to-publish to another publisher.
- You and your colleagues who fit one or more of the above profiles.

Please sign in:

I, _____, am the creator of my work. Whether I write fiction or non-fiction, I am THE expert of my experiences.

My work deserves to be:
- **recognized**
- **celebrated**
- **honored**
- **read**
- **recommended**
- **kept alive**

How Does this Book Work?

Through this workbook, I will be your coach for 22 days. Why 22 days? When you stick to a program for 21 days, you develop new habits. I want you to fortify yourself with new habits, graduate on Day 22, and from that day on... look forward to finding other name-building/platform-building games and thrive as an author.

Is your career worth investing 22 minutes for 22 days? I say YES!

Each day I will give you an exercise or two. In the initial days, I will guide you step by step by giving you examples on the left page; you will use the worksheet on the right page and log the date. If you complete an exercise before 22 minutes, use the remaining minutes to brainstorm other ways to approach the assignment. Please do not "skim or skip" and say you're done before 22 days; remember: the reward is developing new habits after 21 days. Some of my clients stretched the 22 days into a month or even 2 months. Stretch the fun.

(left page)	(right page)
Coach Teresa's Examples	YOUR TURN to DO the EXERCISES

There's no need to badger yourself if you miss a day. However, if you do have to miss a day (let's say you've won the lottery and have to fly out to claim your winnings and you forgot to bring this workbook), I want you to give yourself at least 5 minutes during the day to think about an exercise from a previous day. Write down on a piece of paper: "I particularly liked the _____ _____ exercise(s)."

Day 1, Exercise #1 of 2   Coach Teresa's Example Page

WHO AM I? If I want others to notice me, *I* need to notice myself.

	I am Teresa LeYung Ryan
Themes/Issues /Subject matter I write about:	Modern courageous women unbeknownst to themselves; immigrant experiences; growing up with mental illness in family; child-witness to violence.
What's unique about me?	I'm the only Teresa LeYung Ryan. LeYung is a name I created to honor my maternal & paternal families.
Some books I'd read again and again. Book titles, authors' names and genres	**These works influence my own writing:** *Charlotte's Web* by E.B.White (children); *Woman Warrior* by Maxine Hong Kingston (memoir); *Where the Heart Is* by Billie Letts (novel); *Wordsworth the Poet* by Frances Kakugawa (children); *Lost in Yonkers* by Neil Simon (a play)
Who do I like to hang around with?	My friends & family members who do not judge themselves or others and are supportive of my dreams.
Hobbies that make me happy	Taking photos of friends and colleagues for their personal & business portfolios; preparing simple meals that are tasty & nutritious; making special occasion cards (using my photos and my LOVE MADE OF HEART trademark) for loved ones.
What groups am I a member of?	**writers/other professional organizations/social/community/online** Women's National Book Association; California Writers Club; my mastermind group; writing-buddies; East Bay Regional Park District friends; the Fab Five; critique group; facebook.com; twitter.com; LinkedIn.com; savethelibraries.spaces.live.com; booktour.com; Goodreads.com; Redroom.com; indiebound.org; Librarything.com; savingcinderella.ning.com
My Beliefs & Values	"Everyone deserves to live joyfully. I play a role in world peace by being kind to my neighbors, coworkers, colleagues, friends, family and me."
My Hopes and Dreams	To touch lives with my writing; to receive the Pulitzer prize for a novel, memoir, play or screenplay.

Day 1, Exercise #1 of 2 Today's Date: _____

WHO ARE YOU? If YOU want others to notice YOU, you need to notice yourself.

	I am: _____ (your full name)
Themes/Issues /Subject matter I write about:	
What's unique about me?	
Some books I'd read again and again. Book titles, authors' names & genres	**These works influence my own writing:**
Who do I like to hang around with?	
Hobbies that make me happy	
What groups am I a member of?	writers/other professional organizations/social/community/online Don't forget church, study, job-search groups, and PTA.
My Beliefs & Values	
My Hopes and Dreams	

Day 1, Exercise #2 of 2 "Follow particular footsteps."

I want to build a name for myself; first, let me look at the names of the people I admire. I'm a big fan of:

	Maxine Hong Kingston	Rita Lakin	Ginger Rogers, deceased
What industry is she in?	Books	Books	Movies
What do I think about when I hear her name?	Author of *Woman Warrior*; *Chinaman*; *Fifth Book of Peace*; *To be a Poet*; many others	Author of the Gladdy Gold (70-year-old private investigator) comedy-mystery series; *Getting Old Is A Disaster* is book 5; *Getting Old Is Tres Dangereux* is book 6.	Ballroom dancing; Romantic comedies;
Themes/Issues **What does she symbolize/ represent/ portray/ write about/ speak up for?**	Experiences of Chinese immigrants living in the United States; feminist movement; war veterans	Old age; Laughing at old age; Friendship; Families; Romance; Adventure; History	Working class; Spunky women; Quirky women; Single mothers; Disparity between have and have-nots;
Adjectives to describe her or her protagonists	Gracious; graceful; calm; articulate; quietly powerful	Engaging, funny, warm, confident, prolific writer	Funny, lively, graceful, adorable

What *I* (Teresa) _have in common_ with these 3 super-famous people:
MAXINE: being Chinese-American; write about immigrant experiences.
RITA: Women's National Book Association; blend humor into sobering subjects; protagonists modeled after our mothers.
GINGER: protagonists are funny; quirky; spunky

Day 1, Exercise #2 of 2 Today's Date: _____
"Follow particular footsteps," says Coach Teresa.

YOU want to build a name for yourself; first, let's look at the names of people you admire. You're a big fan of: (these people could be in any industry, however, include at least one author)

	Celebrity #1	Celebrity #2	Celebrity #3
What industry is she/he in?			
What do you think of when you hear her/his name?			
Themes/Issues: What does she/he symbolize/ represent/ portray/ write about/ speak up for?			
Adjectives to describe her/him			

What *YOU have in common* with these 3 super-famous people:

Celebrity#1_____

Celebrity#2_____

Celebrity#3_____

Day 2, Exercise 1 of 2

I research and get more interesting facts about these 3 super-famous people I admire & respect:

	Maxine Hong Kingston	Rita Lakin	Ginger Rogers, deceased
What else is she known for?	Engaging "talk-story"; peace activist; poet; Interviewed by Bill Moyers; National Humanities Medal	Worked on shows such as *Dr. Kildare*, *Peyton Place*, *Mod Squad* & *Dynasty*. Created *The Rookies*, *Flamingo Road* and Nightingales. Wrote many MOWs (Movie's of the Week) and two original theatrical plays.	Her dramatic roles in social issue films: *I'll be Seeing You*; *Primrose Path*; *Storm Warning*; *Twist of Fate*; *Kitty Foyle: The Natural History of a Woman*
Groups/ Organi-zations she asso-ciates with	U.S. Veterans; Amnesty International; University of California, Berkeley; Her publishers; PEN	Women's National Book Association; Mystery Writers of America; Malice Domestic; Sisters In Crime	In 1936 Ginger Rogers was commissioned as the only woman admiral of the Texas Navy. She was a fashion consultant for the JC Penney chain from 1972-75.
A quote from her	"To me success means effectiveness in the world, that I am able to carry my ideas and values into the world -- that I am able to change it in positive ways."	"I write about little old ladies having fun solving mysteries when they might be invisible to the rest of the world."	"The most important thing in anyone's life is to be giving something. The quality I can give is fun, joy and happiness. This is my gift."
Other interesting facts about her	Maxine Hong Kingston began writing at the age of nine ("I was in the fourth grade and all of a sudden this poem started coming out of me").	Rita Lakin, who lives in California, gets the authentic details of the retirement community in Florida (where her protagonist lives) from her friends who live there.	At the age of 14, young Ginger won the Texas State Charleston Championship. In 1984, at age 74, Ginger directed her first stage musical, *Babes In Arms*.

Day 2, Exercise 1 of 2 Today's Date: _____

You research and get more interesting facts about the 3 super-famous people you admire & respect:

	Celebrity #1	Celebrity #2	Celebrity #3
What else is she/he known for?			
Groups/ Organizations she/he associates with			
A quote from her/him			
Other interesting facts about her/him			

Day 2, Exercise 2 of 2

Let's talk, logically. Famous people have other people to identify new fans for them, keep track of their popularity, and continuously build their names.

Guess what? You can do all that for yourself (identify your new fans; keep track of your popularity, and continuously build your name). And, because YOU are THE expert of your own experiences and desires, you're the ideal person for this job.

I have discovered secret keys to accomplish the job with ease. Before I pass the keys to you, I want to show you something. I Googled the 3 people I admire & respect (each name inside quotation marks), recorded the number of search results, and kept notes for myself.

	Google Search Results	Notes of Interest
Celebrity #1	"Maxine Hong Kingston" 276,000 search results.	This means Maxine's name appears in 276,000 webpages.
Celebrity #2	"Rita Lakin" 47,400 results Rita is the creator of the Gladdy Gold comedy-mystery series.	"Rita Lakin" results would probably be 10 x 47,400 if search engines served us during Rita's previous career (when she worked on television shows such as *Dr. Kildare*, *Peyton Place*, *Mod Squad*, *Dynasty*, and more) **ritalakin.com**
Celebrity #3	"Ginger Rogers" 625,000 results.	That many results! Even though Ms. Rogers died in 1995 at the age of 83, she still has a huge following. Her <u>name</u> lives on!

Day 2, Exercise 2 of 2 Today's Date: _____

Google the 3 people YOU admire & respect (be sure to put each name inside quotation marks), record the number of search results, and keep notes of interest.

	Google Search Results	Notes of Interest
Celebrity #1 " "		
Celebrity #2 " "		
Celebrity #3 " "		

Google **YOUR own name** inside quotation marks:
Are there other people who have your name?
How many search results are you? _____

- Please do not let the number discourage you if it doesn't meet your expectations. The exercises in this workbook will help you grow that number.
- If you are thrilled with the number, take a look at who the websites belong to. These are your fans or prospective fans.
- Keep track of "numbers/counts." How many visitors go to your website, blog, YouTube channel, etc.? We'll make those numbers grow too.

Day 3   Cyberspace You Say?   Today's Date:_____
Exercise 1 of 2
If you don't already understand the workings of websites/blogs, please get onto the Internet, and look at your computer/laptop screen while studying this section. Even if you already understand the terminology and navigating shortcuts, read this section anyway.

Definitions below are from <u>http://www.thefreedictionary.com</u>

World Wide Web (*Abbr.* **WWW**) = The complete set of documents residing on all Internet servers, accessible to users via a simple point-and-click system.

Internet = An interconnected system of networks that connects computers around the world via the TCP/IP protocol (http://   )

Browser = A program that accesses and displays files and other data available on the WWW.
Examples: Mozilla Firefox; Internet Explorer; Safari

Mozilla Firefox	Internet Explorer	Safari

Which browser do you use? _____
If you're using someone else's computer, what browser does the owner use? _____

Search Engine = A computer program that retrieves documents or files or data from a database or from a computer network (especially from the Internet). The top 3 search engines used in 2009/2010 are: **Google; Yahoo; Bing.**
Which search engine do you often use? _____

The visual shows my using Mozilla Firefox for browser and Google for search engine.

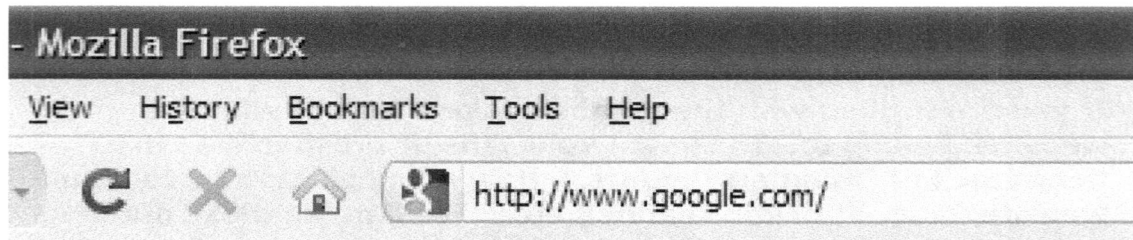

URL = Acronym for <u>U</u>niform <u>R</u>esource <u>L</u>ocator = **the address to a webpage** on the **WWW**.

Examples: **The URL for Google is: http://Google.com**

The URL for Yahoo is: http://Yahoo.com

The visual to the right shows what I see on my monitor when I key in **http://LoveMadeOfHeart.com** (the URL) into the **address-window** of Mozilla Firefox browser.

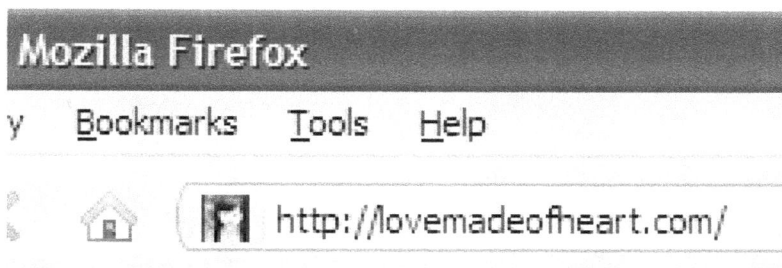

After I press the enter key on my keyboard and the home page of my website appears, I click on **"Reviews/Interviews"** (a tab at left margin of website).

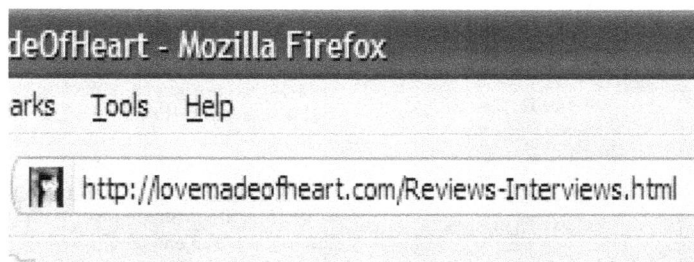

See how the URL in the address-window reflects what page I'm looking at?

Let's say I want to find Maxine Hong Kingston's website but I don't know the URL (address of her website). Below, I'm using Mozilla Firefox browser and Google search engine to find webpages that have the words "Maxine Hong Kingston" Maxine doesn't have a website, but there are many websites with pages about her. The first search result is from Wikipedia.org

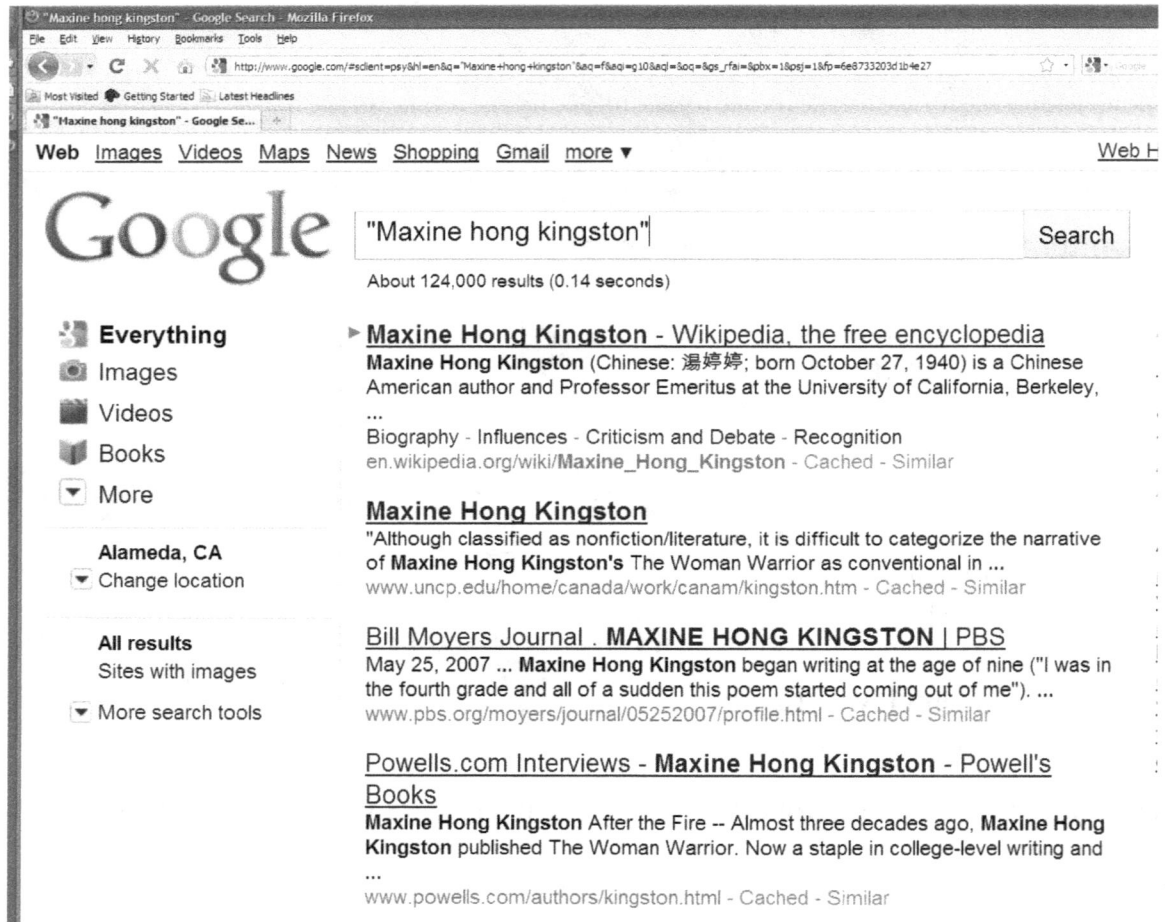

Cyberspace = The electronic medium of computer networks, in which online communication takes place.

Blog abbreviation for we**blog (a blog is a website)**
Verb: To write **posts** (entries) in, add material to, or maintain a weblog.
Noun: A shared on-line journal where you can publish your **posts** (entries about your experiences, observations, expertise, and hobbies); the most recently published post appears first to readers; readers are given the opportunity to submit comments.

The visual below shows my keying in the URL **http://writingcoachteresa.com** into the **address-window** of Mozilla Firefox browser. Then, if I press the enter key on my keyboard, cyberspace forwards that URL to my primary URL
http://LoveMadeOfHeart.com because I have asked my webmaster Linda Lee to "point" my domain name of **writingcoachteresa.com** to **LoveMadeOfHeart.com.** I do that so that I have only one website to keep track of. I have several other domain names (including **TeresaLeYungRyan.com**) that are pointed to **LoveMadeOfHeart.com.**

I love to blog. Why? Because I like to be in control of what to publish and when to publish.

Exercise 2 of 2
When you're at http://LoveMadeOfHeart.com, click on [**TERESA'S BLOG**] at left margin. When you get to my blog, look for the empty box above the word "search." Then key in the words and question mark: **What is a blog?** into that search box; then press your enter key; let my blog find my **post** (journal entry/column/article) that contains those 4 words/**tag**: What is a blog

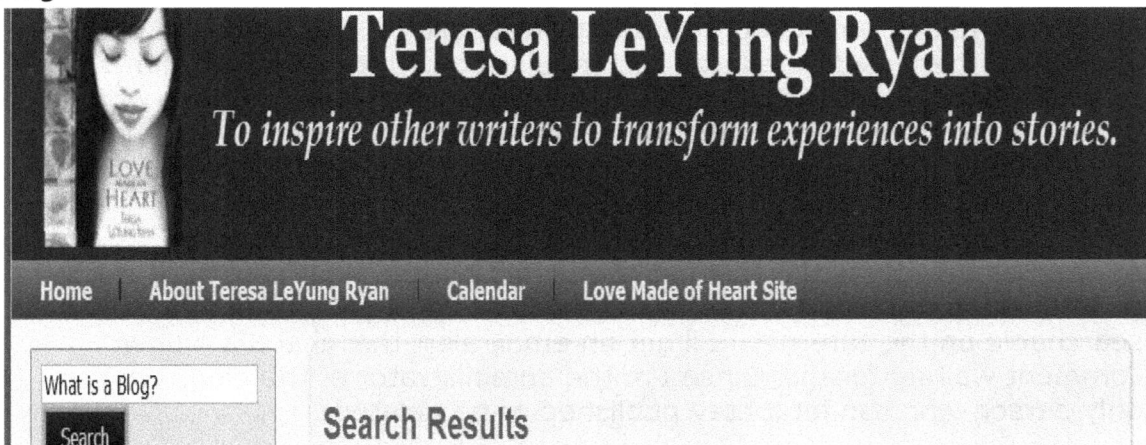

Teresa LeYung Ryan
To inspire other writers to transform experiences into stories.

| Home | About Teresa LeYung Ryan | Calendar | Love Made of Heart Site |

What is a Blog?
Search

Search Results

You're seeing just the abstract of this post. To see the entire post, click on the blue title-bar: **What is a Blog? And Why?**

Read the post. Then . . .

Scroll down your screen until you see the boxes to Leave a Reply.

Leave a Reply

	Name
	Mail (will not be published)
	Website

Submit Comment

Fill in your name, email address, and website/blog URL if you have one of your own. Then inside the large rectangular box, write your comment. What to say? Tell the world what issues/subject matter/themes you are writing about. Sign off with your full name as you would in a letter (even though you keyed in your name in the small box). Why? Let readers see your name again, especially near your own statements.

As soon as you press the [submit comment] button, your comment will be **published** in my blog (which means the content of your comment will be searchable on the Internet. I'll get an email alert that there is a new comment waiting for me. Since I'm the administrator of the blog, I'm the only person who can let it stay published or be deleted.

Search engines and the Internet work fast these days. After you submit your comment. Go to Google.com

In the Google search box, enter your name (the way you signed off in the comment box of my blog) and a phrase you used in your comment. Press the enter key on your keyboard and let Google begin searching.

See how combination of tags (your name + keywords or key phrases) will guide the search engines? Amazing.

To get comfortable submitting comments, use the search box in my blog to find posts.
Example: You could key in the words: **book festival**. Then press the search button. See the 4 posts that contain those 2 words **book** and **festival** (not necessarily together). However, if you add quotation marks in the search box: **"book festival"** you'll get the 2 posts that contain the combination and sequence of those two words (a targeted search).

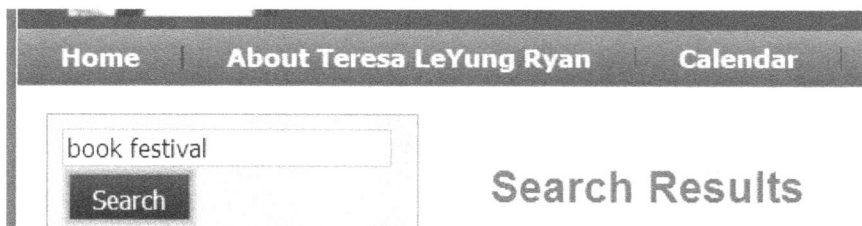

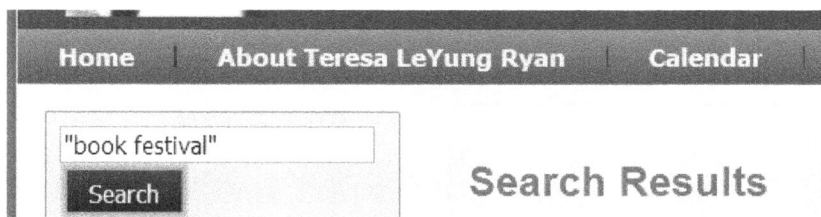

Day 4 To Be a Blogger Today's Date: _____

If you want to have your own blog (free)... Please go to http://wordpress.com   and sign up for a free blog. All you need is an email address. http://wordpress.**com** blogs are free.

If you already have a website and want to add a blog-component to it, ask your webmaster to help you. If you are the webmaster and need help, go to http://www.askmepc-webdesign.com/ and ask Linda Lee (my web coach) to help.

In any event, get started with a free blog (to get the practice).
Your blog = a body of work that *you* publish on cyberspace.

On the **http://wordpress.com** home page, click on the "**Sign up now**" button.

Express yourself.
Start a blog.

Sign up now

You'll see a page like this one:

Be selective in choosing a blog name. Blog "usernames" (like URLs) cannot have spaces; use letters and numbers only. If the username you want is already taken by someone else, consider adding a word (such as: writer or author or books or writings or blog). Example above shows my choosing WritingCoachTeresa as my username.

Read Wordpress.com's "terms of service" and check their box if you agree. Write down your username and password somewhere (unless you know you won't forget) before you click on "gimme a blog" and the "next" button.

Remember to look at your screen for helpful prompts from Wordpress.com. After you sign up for a free blog, they will email you with further instructions.

Here's what my blog at wordpress.com looks like after I log in with my password. I am the Site Administrator. I have access to the "Dashboard" (the control panel). Visitors cannot see my dashboard. Please do <u>not</u> give out your password to anyone unless you want that person to be able to control the dashboard too.

The Dashboard shows me how many posts I have published on this blog; how many categories I have created; how many "tags" I have used/saved; how many comments I have received from visitors; recent drafts by me; and more.

The icons on the left margin are "navigating" buttons. For example: If I want to write a new post, I would click on the icon that looks like a push-pin.

Writing Coach Teresa's Blog — Visit Site

🏠 Dashboard

WordPress announcement: <u>Posterous Importer</u>

Right Now

At a Glance

23	Posts	16	Comments
1	Page	3	Approved
4	Categories	0	Pending
478	Tags	13	Spam

Cyberspace guru Linda Lee created <u>http://wordpresscentral.org/</u> to show new bloggers how to set up their blogs. Watch the videos.

Day 4 Continuing   Today's Date: _____

Here's what my blog at wordpress.com look like from a visitor's point of view. **http://writingcoachteresa.wordpress.com** **(I created this blog in Dec. 2009)**

In the search box, key in: Writing Resolutions

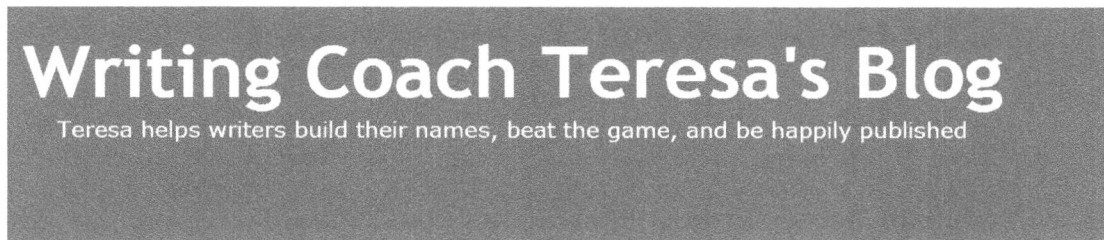

Writing Coach Teresa's Blog
Teresa helps writers build their names, beat the game, and be happily published

Search Results   writing resolutions|

Then press the enter key. There are 5 search results – 5 posts with the tags: writing resolutions

If you had keyed in those 2 tags inside quotation marks "writing resolutions" and pressed the enter key, my blog would show "no post found" because I haven't used those two words (together, in that order) in any of my posts (at least not as of December 2010).

For this exercise: after you've found the 5 posts that contain the tags [**writing resolutions],** click on the post entitled: My Writer's Resolutions for this Month or Year.

Key in your full name (or your pen name), email address, your URL (the address of *your* blog/website); and use the big box to declare your resolutions. Before you press the [submit] key...

Save a copy of what you keyed into this box. [If you don't know how to use the toolbar on your computer screen to copy and paste text, try this: use your mouse to highlight the text; then press these 2 keys [Ctrl] [C] at the same time (this action serves as "copy"). To paste the copied text into another document, press these 2 keys [Ctrl] [V] at the same time.

Day 5   Today's Date: _____

Coach Teresa, tell me about tags.

Read this page and the next two.

Tags are words and phrases. When you understand the 'function' of tags, you will smile. Where do we see tags?

Analogy #1 You walk into a supermarket, looking for toothpaste. You look at the signs over the aisles. You see it-- the sign "Personal Hygiene." "Personal Hygiene" is a tag. Tags help us find things.

Analogy #2 You're looking for a particular book in the library. If such a book is shelved and someone has cataloged it, then, you'd be able to find it if you know one or more pieces of information about the book.
- **Author's name?** E. B. White
- **Book title?** *Charlotte's Web*
- **Subject matter?** **children's book** about a pig and a spider

E.B. White; Charlotte's Web; children's book about a pig and a spider (these words/phrases are all tags). Tags help us find books.

Tags (keywords & key phrases) help us find anything and everything that is "cataloged" or "indexed" on the Internet.

Example: You want to know where the nearest library is. Inside the search box (Google, Yahoo, others), you key in the word [library] and your zip code, and you press the enter key. Voila! The search engine shows you a list of libraries near you. The word library and your zip code – they are tags.

Let's say I'm on the Internet looking for a book that a friend is recommending. What if I didn't know the author's name or the title of the book? All I know is that there's this great children's story about a pig and a spider. What if I didn't know about the pig or the spider; I only knew I wanted "something" to help my child understand the cycle of life or a child helping an animal or about animals on a farm or about helping a friend. The words I key into the search engine box are "tags."

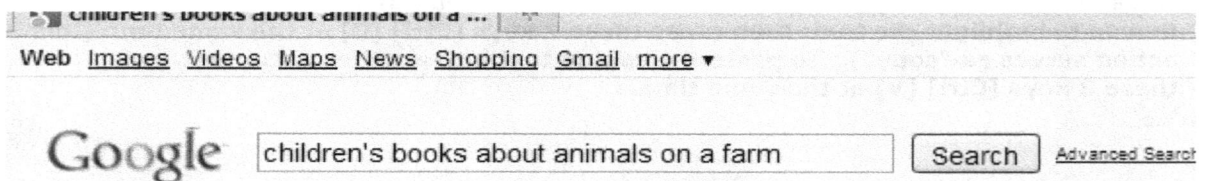

children's books about animals on a ...	
Web Images Videos Maps News Shopping Gmail more ▼	

Google | children's books about animals on a farm | Search | Advanced Search

Day 5   Coach Teresa, continue telling me more about Tags.

Let's turn the table on tags.

You want people to find you *and your book*.

More specific--You want people who don't already know you *or the existence of your book* to find you *and your book*.

Even more specific—You want people who want or need the information/subject matters/themes in your book to find *you and your book*.

Secret Key #1: Identify the tags that people might use to look for the information/subject matters/themes that happen to be in your book.

What words/phrases might they key in their Search boxes?

While your target-consumers are looking for something else on the Internet, they find <u>you</u> by accident (through the tags they key in and those *you* key into your webpage and webpage description and blog posts). I, Coach Teresa, call this "Accidental Matching." How wonderful for the people who find you by accident; how wonderful for you to gain new fans.

So, if your prospective fans don't know your name or that you have written a book or books they would embrace, and, if your work is not cataloged/indexed (tagged) in the World Wide Web . . . how would anyone find you? It would be as if your book is sitting on a library shelf, hiding behind many other books, and, no one has created catalog cards for you or entered your book profile in the database.

I would like to hear from you. Check in with Coach Teresa. Go to my main website/blog http://writingcoachTeresa.com (this URL could take you to another URL). Wherever this URL takes you, click on the [TERESA'S BLOG] tab. Then in my blog's search box, key in these words inside quotation marks: "Day 5 of 22"   Tell me what "tags" *you* came up with. Then read the next page.

Day 5 Coach Teresa, *show* me more about Tags.

**Let's try and find that children's book I was looking for.
I key in 4 words inside Google search box:
children's book pig spider**

See how the search engine found website pages that contain those 4 words (tags: children's   book   pig   spider)?

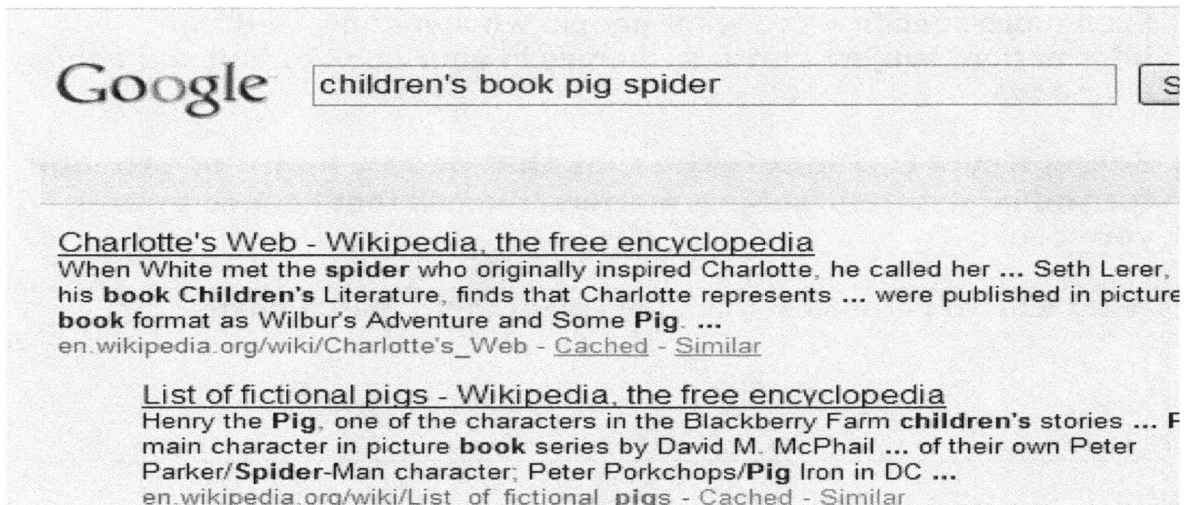

Google · children's book pig spider

Charlotte's Web - Wikipedia, the free encyclopedia
When White met the **spider** who originally inspired Charlotte, he called her ... Seth Lerer, his **book Children's** Literature, finds that Charlotte represents ... were published in picture **book** format as Wilbur's Adventure and Some **Pig**. ...
en.wikipedia.org/wiki/Charlotte's_Web - Cached - Similar

List of fictional pigs - Wikipedia, the free encyclopedia
Henry the **Pig**, one of the characters in the Blackberry Farm **children's** stories ... F main character in picture **book** series by David M. McPhail ... of their own Peter Parker/**Spider**-Man character; Peter Porkchops/**Pig** Iron in DC ...
en.wikipedia.org/wiki/List_of_fictional_pigs - Cached - Similar

Secret Key #1 into the lock:

Look at the websites that have all 4 words I keyed in the search box. Someone from each of those sites had to place those exact words (tags) so that search engines would find those words.   Possessing and broadcasting the right combination of words attract people who are looking for that same combination.

All the words and phrases that are keyed in as tags on websites/blogs (by you and other owners of websites/blogs) = indexes of all the documents in those websites/blogs that are on the World Wide Web.

And, how many ways can people find you? The more specific (and the more frequent) you use your tags to describe your work, the better the odds that your tags will lead people to your site. When people find your tags, they find YOU.

Day 6   Today's Date: _____

Coach Teresa's Example Page – My Tags

Why do I like "tags" ? I get to be a match-maker.

These are some tags that best identify who I am:

- **Teresa LeYung Ryan (my name)**
- *Love Made of Heart* **(my first novel's book title)**
- *Build Your Writer's Platform & Fanbase in 22 Days: Attract Agents, Editors, Publishers, Readers, and Media Attention NOW* **(this workbook's title)**
- **Asian American (a group/category)**
- **Chinese American (more targeted than "Asian American")**
- **Chinese American woman (more targeted than "Chinese American")**
- **Chinese American woman writer (combination of tags that describes me)**

These are some tags that best identify the groups and themes I write about:

- **Chinese Americans**
- **Chinese American women**

- **Immigrant stories**
- **Chinese Immigrant stories**
- **Chinese immigrant mother/daughter**
- **Stigmas and Chinese immigrants (an issue)**

- **Stigmas of Mental illness (an issue)**
- **Survivors of war and mental illness (a group linked to an issue)**
- **Women survivors of war and mental illness (a more targeted group linked to an issue)**

Some Tags "synonymous" with My Writing:

Chinese Immigrants in U.S.A.	Chinese immigrant mothers-daughters	Mental illness stigmas	Immigrant Mothers & mental illness	Survivors of war	Survivors of war & Mental illness

Day 6 YOUR TURN   Today's Date_____

To be a match-maker with tags. Secret Key #1

What are some tags that best identify who YOU are?

- (your name)
-
-
-
-
-
-

What are some tags that best identify the groups and themes YOU write about?

-
-
-
-
-

Some Tags "synonymous" with Your Writing:

Day 6

> **Author:** "I've written a book."
> **Publisher:** "Wonderful. Who will you market your book to?"
> **Author:** "Everyone!"
> **Publisher:** "Everyone?"
> **Ask yourself these questions:**
> Do I buy *every* genre?
> Do I pay attention to every news item/subject matter?
> Do certain voices/personalities hook me?
> If I get to choose what and who to pay attention to, then, all my prospective fans have the same rights and prerogatives, don't they?

Secret Key #2:
Identifying my prospective audience
(Who can relate to me?)

Who am I?
- I am a Chinese-American woman who writes about my family's immigrant experiences (a factor that influences my writing)
- I am an adult-daughter of a parent who suffered mental illness (another factor that influences my writing)
- I was a child-witness to violence (a third factor that influences my writing)

Let's take a closer look at my first bullet-point: I am a Chinese-American woman who writes about my family's immigrant experiences.

I Google the question: How many Chinese Americans live in USA?
The URL (webpage) below was a result of the search:
http://usa.usembassy.de/society-demographics.htm
According to the 2000 Census, 12.7 million Asians and Pacific Islanders live in the United States of America. **2.7 million of the 12.7 million reported as Chinese. 50 percent of the Asians resided in three states: California, New York and Hawaii.** Two of these states had Asian populations exceeding 1 million: California (4.2 million) and New York (1.2 million).

Question to Self: Do I fantasize about "everyone" reading my book(s) or do I reach out and invest my energy in building my name among the Chinese-American or Asian-American communities (who are more likely to relate to me)? Hmm... I live in California; there are 4.2 million Asian-Americans in my state. Not all of these folks are immigrants, but, they are descendents of immigrants. Wow, if my voice could hook even 10% of 4.2 million, that would be 420,000 prospective readers!

Day 6 YOUR TURN   **Today's Date**_____

Secret Key #2:
Identifying YOUR prospective audience
(Who can relate to YOU?)

Who are YOU?

- I am _____ who write about

_____

- I am/was _____

- I am/was _____

Let's take a closer look at the **first bullet-point**: I am _____

Who can relate to me or what I write about? (Group 1) _____

Where are these folks? _____

Question to Self: Instead of spreading myself thin marketing to "everyone" on this planet, do I **reach out** and invest my energy in building my name among

_____ ? If my voice could hook this group, that could be _____ prospective readers!

Let's take a closer look at the **second bullet-point**: I am _____

Who can relate to me? (Group 2) _____

Where are these folks? _____

Let's take a closer look at the **third bullet-point**: I am _____

Who can relate to me? (Group 3) _____

Where are these folks? _____

Probably there is overlap in the numbers from Groups 1, 2, and 3; these are the folks who can relate to me not only in one aspect, but also in two or three aspects. These are my target-readers. Wow!

Day 7 Exercise 1 of 2 Today's Date_____

Today we are going to look at what you've discovered about yourself from the preceding exercises.

My name is synonymous with these themes (findings from Day 6):

_____

_____

_____

What these famous people and I have in common (findings from Day 1):

_____-_____

_____-_____

_____-_____

These groups are my prospective fans/readers (findings from Day 6):

_____

_____

_____

My hopes & dreams (from Day 1):

_____

_____

_____

_____

Day 7 Exercise 2 of 2 Today's Date_____

Time to reach out. **Now that you know how to find people and information by keying "tags" in Google.com or Yahoo.com (or other search engines), find the website of one famous person whom you respect and admire, get his/her contact info, and write an email to let him or her know how much you enjoy/appreciate/have studied his or her work.**

This person doesn't have to be an author. Look at the names you listed on Day 1. The celebrity may not get to read your message, or, if the celebrity doesn't offer a forum for comments, you go ahead and publish your note on your own sites; the importance is that you are reaching out to introduce yourself.

Who will you write to? What will you say? Be brief. Be sincere.

> If you're going to email the celebrity, email yourself first. What does the email look like? Is there a subject line?
> Is your message one *l o n g* paragraph that takes up the entire screen? Before you press the "send" button to the celebrity, add yourself to cc or bcc (bcc means that people you're sending the email to and the people cc'ed will not be able to see who you are bcc'ing). When I'm emailing a group of people, I put addresses in bcc so that the recipients won't see the long string of names & addresses (also a way to protect everyone's addresses)
> If the celebrity you're writing to has the kind of website that requires you to fill out a form and you cannot cc or bcc yourself, then, copy the text and keep a record of when you submitted the form and what you said.
> Keep an electronic copy of everything you write and send. You're building a repertoire of important documents. If you don't have a memory stick to store documents, then email documents to yourself and move those emails to a folder (if your email service has that feature).

Here's what I wrote to Maxine Hong Kingston in 1995

Dear Maxine,
I've been too shy to write to you, but, when my colleague in my critique group told me about your teaching at UC I knew this was an opportunity to tell you how your book ***Woman Warrior*** changed my life five years ago. I laughed and cried, mostly cried with your protagonist. I thought that I was the only Chinese-American girl who felt *that* angry while growing up. Your book has inspired me to write about my family, and, I hope that someday my work will touch readers the way your story has touched me. Thank you for writing such powerful words.
Sincerely,
Teresa LeYung Ryan
[I would have added my website URL and email address if I had them then. I hand-wrote the letter and mailed it to Maxine at her U.C. Berkeley address. By the way, I didn't expect to receive a reply. But Maxine replied! She sent me a hand-written note, wishing me success and giving me her agent's name!]

Day 8   Today's Date_____

Celebrities Reach Out; I Reach Out. Reaching out is easy and fun if you know what you want.

Yesterday, you reached out to one of your favorite celebrities. Celebrities use their status to speak out on issues and help organizations whose mission statements match up with their messages.

Most authors of non-fiction know the importance of being recognized as an expert in subject matters *they* write about.

Authors of fiction also need to acknowledge themselves as experts in the subject matters *they* write about in order to gain recognition.

In Google.com, key in the name of one of your favorite celebrities and the word charity.
Or go to   http://www.looktothestars.org/celebrity/

Look at the list of the charity organizations that your favorite celebrities cheer for. Do any of these organizations connect with what <u>you're writing about</u>? If yes, fill in the blanks below:

<u>Celebrity</u>	<u>Name of Organization</u> and	<u>Keywords in Mission Statement</u>
_____	_____	_____
_____	_____	_____
_____	_____	_____

Even if none of the organizations connect with your subject matters, fill in the above blanks for 2 organizations you recognize. The point is for you to see the keywords used by these organizations. Pay attention to the subjects, action verbs, and objects in the sentences in their mission statements.

Authors of fiction, memoirs, and creative non-fiction: Remember that you are THE experts of your experiences. The themes/subject matters in your stories make you the authorities and prospective spokespeople for non-fiction issues.

Day 9   Today's Date: _____
Small/Big Organizations Reach Out; I Reach Out

Organizations reach out to celebrities who can broadcast their mission statements because celebrity-voices attract media attention.

How would I, an author, attract attention?
Secret Key #3
By being consistent with my words. By creating and broadcasting *my mission statement* and linking it to organizations that speak the same words.

Coach Teresa's Example:

On Day 6, I identified the groups and themes I write about, and, I identified my prospective audience/fans/readers (people who can relate to me).

One theme that I write about is: mental illness + the stigmas

Now I need to <u>link the nouns with verbs</u> in order to create *my* mission statement. If I am THE expert of my experiences / an authority of the subject matters I write about, then what is my mission?

I go to Google.com and typed in the words stigmas mental illness in the search box. Below are the search results on the first page. I <u>focus on the action-verbs and powerful phrases</u>.

• <u>**Mental health: Overcoming the *stigma* of *mental illness* ...**</u>

Mental health — **Understand and overcome** the *stigma* of *mental illness* and mental health disorders.
*www.mayoclinic.com/health/**mental**-health/MH00076*

- *Mental* Health Matters

Stigma is really about disrespect and dehumanization. It is giving someone with a *mental illness* a label and treating them differently based on that label. **...** *www.dupagehealth.org/mental_health/stigma.html -*

- ## Glenn Close: *Mental Illness*: The *Stigma* of Silence

Oct 21, 2009 **...** It is an odd paradox that a society, which can now speak openly and unabashedly about topics that were once unspeakable, still remains **...** *www.huffingtonpost.com/.../mental-illness-the-stigma_b_328591.html -*

- NAMI: National Alliance on *Mental Illness* | Fight *Stigma*

Access More Anti-*Stigma* Resources. Discover In Our Own Voice, a powerful anti-*stigma* tool to **change hearts, minds, and attitudes** about *mental illness* **...** *www.nami.org/template.cfm?Section...Stigma... -*

I click on the links to read more and to find more action-verbs and power-phrases.

- **overcome** the many **misconceptions**
- Help **dispel myths** about mental illness.
- **Promote greater awareness** of mental illness.
- **Ms. Glenn Close** says in her article for *The Huffington Post*: "Over the last year, I have worked with some visionary groups to start http://BringChange2Mind.org an organization that **strives to inspire people to start talking openly** about mental illness, to **break through the silence and fear**.
- **NAMI** – National Alliance on Mental Illness. **StigmaBusters** is a **network of dedicated advocates** across the country and around the world who **seek to fight inaccurate and hurtful representations of mental illness**.

Oh! I know that Carmen Lee, a fellow member of California Writers Club, is the founder of Stamp Out Stigma. So, I Google: Stamp Out Stigma mental illness and these results appear:

- *Stamp Out Stigma* | Famous People

Stamp Out Stigma. **Many of the world's most famous, creative, and influential people have had a *mental illness*. The list includes writers, entertainers, ...**
http://www.stampoutstigma.net/famous.html-

- Welcome to *Stamp Out Stigma* Home Page

Welcome to *Stamp Out Stigma,* **a community advocacy and educational outreach program** dedicated to eradicating the *stigma* associated with *mental illness.* **...**
http://www.stampoutstigma.net/

Wow! All these people are helping me choose power-words. After many drafts, I've got it. Here goes . . . my mission statement:

Through my book *Love Made of Heart*, I inspire adult children of mentally-ill parents to speak openly about the stigmas suffered by their parents.

With my mission statement, I am not *just* another author with yet another book. I am *Teresa LeYung Ryan* who uses her book to inspire adult children of mentally-ill parents to speak openly about the stigmas suffered by their parents.

Day 9   Today's Date: _____

Small/Big Organizations Reach Out; YOU Reach Out

YOUR TURN

On Day 6, YOU identified the groups and themes YOU write about. Also, YOU identified YOUR prospective audience/fans/readers (people who can relate to YOU).

One theme that YOU write about is:

_____

Go to Google.com and typed in the words that describe your theme _____ in the search box. Look at the URLs. What are the organizations? Go to their websites. What are their mission statements? Make a list of the <u>action-verbs</u> and <u>powerful phrases</u> they use. If you find articles, look for mentioning of organizations; look for the <u>action-verbs</u> and <u>powerful phrases</u> in the articles too.

Name of Organization & Website Or Author of Articles & Publication's Website	Action-Verbs & Powerful Phrases

This exercise continues on next page . . .

Day 9   Today's Date: _____

If this exercise takes more than 22 minutes, either give yourself more time today OR continue tomorrow. It's fine to invest more days on yourself. Log real date (If you started this exercise on January 9 and continued on January 10, log each date)

Look at one more:

Name of Organization & Website Or Author of Articles & Publication's Website	Action-Verbs & Powerful Phrases

Secret Key #3
Now, <u>link the nouns with verbs</u> in order to create *your* mission statement. If you are THE expert of your experiences / an authority of the subject matters you write about, then what is your mission?

Compose YOUR mission statement:

_____

_____

_____

_____

How do YOU feel about your mission statement?

_____

Day 10 Exercise 1 of 4   Today's Date: _____

Here's my mission statement for my novel: **What's *your* mission statement?**

Through my book *Love Made of Heart*, I inspire adult-children of mentally-ill parents to speak openly about the stigmas their parents suffer.	

Places to show Who YOU Are & What YOU Do (Your Mission Statement)

In Emails.
What does your signature-block say about you now? Anything? Do you use quotes from other people in your signature block? Unless you're writing a book about those people, please stop it. It's time to quote yourself!

You can have multiple versions of your signature block. Choose what you want to advertise in each email. Also, keep your email brief and use bullet points.

	YOUR TURN
Sincerely, Teresa LeYung Ryan http://LoveMadeOfHeart.com Teresa@LoveMadeOfHeart.com I use my book ***Love Made of Heart*** to **inspire** adult-children of mentally-ill parents to speak openly about the stigmas their parents suffer.	

Your turn again: **When you're replying to an email and your signature block is bounced to the bottom of the email string, move it up to where it ought to be—at the end of your reply. Keep your mission statement visible. Golden rule in advertising: show show show, again and again and again.**

Day 10 Exercise 2 of 4 Today's Date: _____

More Places to Show/Broadcast Your Mission Statement:
On envelopes and stationery. On facebook, twitter, LinkedIn, YouTube, and <u>any place that keeps count of your popularity</u>. On Goodreads.com, Librarything.com, and any other groups/sites you named on Day 1 and have joined since then.

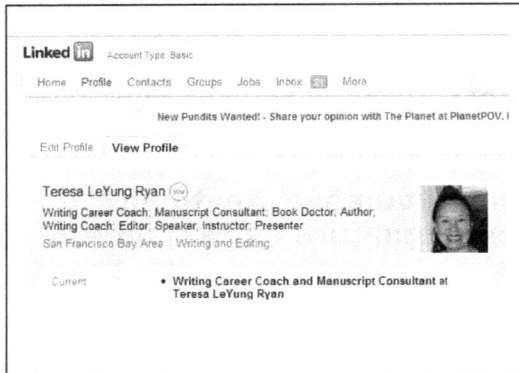

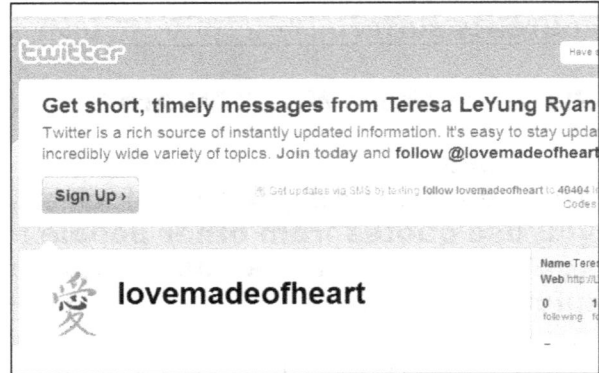

Teresa LeYung Ryan
http://WritingCoachTeresa.com

"Through my workbook, *Build Your Writer's Platform & Fanbase in 22 Days*, I help writers gain visibility before the book is published."

Sincerely,

"Coach Teresa"
Teresa LeYung Ryan

WritingCoachTeresa@Gmail.com

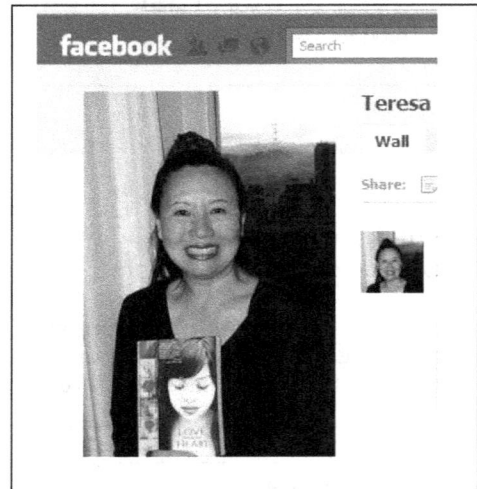

Get a ream of high-quality paper and make your own stationery.

What about your out-going message on voicemail? At least give out your website address. Here's mine: "This is Writing-Career-Coach Teresa LeYung Ryan. Have you seen my new workbook ***Build Your Writer's Platform & Fanbase in 22 Days***? My websites are **WritingCoachTeresa.com & 22DaysToBuildPlatform.com** Happy name building!"

Day 10 Exercise 3 of 4 Today's Date: _____

Go back and review Day 4. You had submitted a comment (your resolutions) to my blog post. Your turn to be the site administrator of your own blog. If you don't already have a blog (you might have one in your website and not know it... ask your webmaster) **or** if you have neither a blog nor a website, then please use the remainder of today and even tomorrow and go to **http://wordpress.com** and **re-read Day 4**.

After you log-in and see your Dashboard, hover your mouse over the icons on the left margin until you find the icon for "settings." Then click on "general." See the Tagline box? You want the tagline to reflect your mission statement.

I have several mission statements, each one specific to the book/service I am offering.

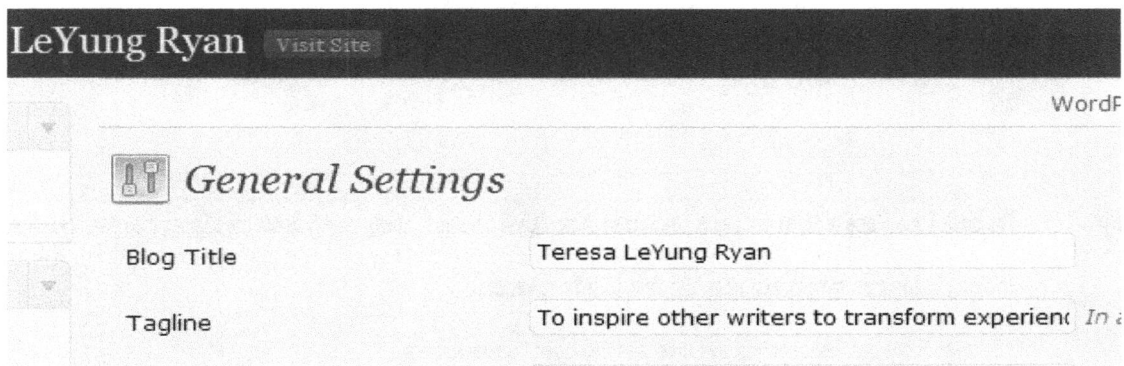

You could change your tagline (mission statement) anytime by following the instructions above. Here are my top 3 taglines/mission statements:

- **I, Teresa LeYung Ryan, shed light on the secret agonies suffered by immigrant women, men and children.**
- **I, Teresa LeYung Ryan, use my novels to inspire understanding of mental illness/traumas of the mind.**
- **I, Teresa LeYung Ryan, help survivors of violence find their own voices through writing.**

☐ **check box after you've added <u>your</u> mission statement to your blog tagline.**

Day 10 Exercise 4 of 4 Today's Date: _____

If you have a website, update the description for each webpage. You can do this ONLY if you have the software that was used to create your website. Or, you can ask your webmaster to show you what the descriptions look like now; then you provide him/her updated descriptions. I encourage you to take control of your site. Make minor changes yourself; keep your site updated.

Here's my mission statement in the description of the webpage for my novel *Love Made of Heart*:

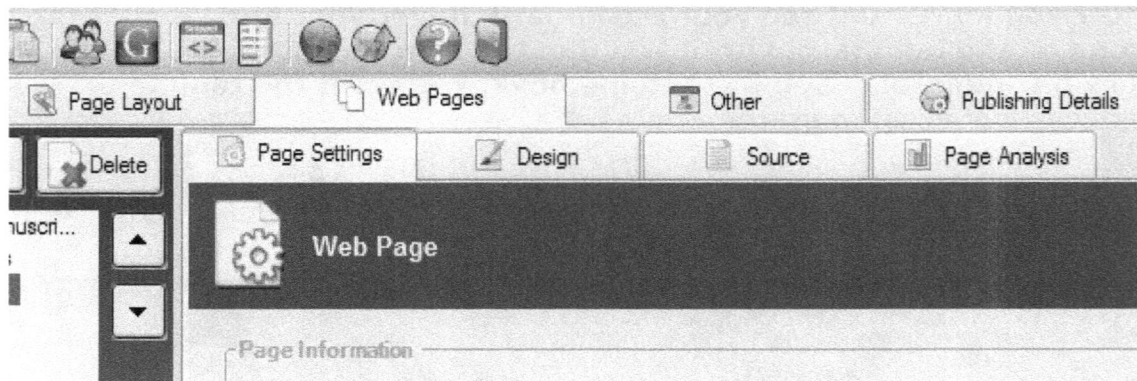

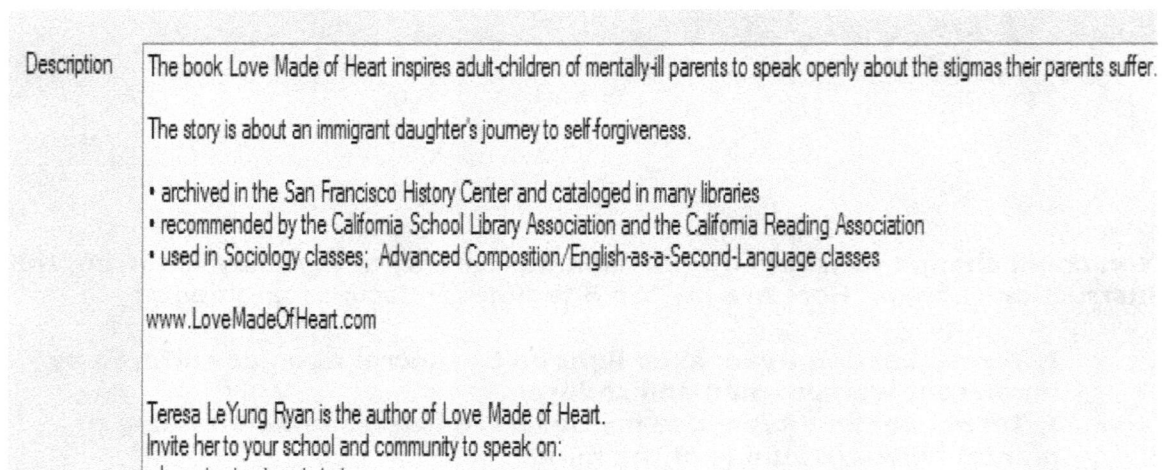

Description

The book Love Made of Heart inspires adult-children of mentally-ill parents to speak openly about the stigmas their parents suffer.

The story is about an immigrant daughter's journey to self-forgiveness.

• archived in the San Francisco History Center and cataloged in many libraries
• recommended by the California School Library Association and the California Reading Association
• used in Sociology classes; Advanced Composition/English-as-a-Second-Language classes

www.LoveMadeOfHeart.com

Teresa LeYung Ryan is the author of Love Made of Heart.
Invite her to your school and community to speak on:

☐   **check box after you've added your mission statement to your webpage(s) descriptions.**

Day 11   Today's Date: _____

Secret Key #4
Link Your NAME to Other People's BOOKS

Do you write non-fiction or fiction that requires *a lot* of research?

If your answer is "yes," consider this: No one knows how much work you've put into your project until they look at your bibliography. **I say** let's use your bibliography to attract attention <u>before</u> your book is published. *I say* you can build your name by writing a sentence or two about each book you've used in your research while writing yours. **List at least 3 of the books from your bibliography:**

If you think that your non-fiction or fiction requires *no* research, <u>think</u> <u>again</u>. Even if you're writing an autobiography, do NOT rely on memory alone or hearsay. Because you'd want to use authentic details and also conduct fact-checking, make a list of the books that would help with fact-checking (dates, names, laws, descriptions for settings) and the books that carry the same themes as yours. How about the books you've read that have influenced or inspired you to write yours? **Create your bibliography here:**

I would like to hear from you. Go to my main website/blog http://writingcoachTeresa.com (this URL could take you to another URL). Wherever this URL takes you, click on the [**TERESA'S BLOG**] tab. Then in my blog's search box, key in these words inside quotation marks: **"Day 11 of 22"   Give me at least 3 book titles that will be in your bibliography. Then read the next 2 pages.**

Day 11
Where to publish your bibliography?

Of course on your own website and blog. Be sure to put the keywords in the tag box in blogs.

☐ **check box after you've done this.**

Secret Key #5

Writing words-of-praise for some of the books in your bibliography. On your website/blog; on booksellers' websites if their sites offer comment boxes; on the authors' or their publishers' sites; and libraries' sites (where *your* future fans now go to look for books similar yours).

By the way, booksellers call these words-of-praise (or criticism) "customer reviews." On some sites, you have to be a member or customer in order to submit "customer reviews." Example: If you wish to write book reviews on Amazon.com, you do have to have an Amazon account, but, you don't have to buy books from them in order to write the reviews.

More Tips and Links to Sites:

- Ask your favorite independent bookseller if they publish readers' reviews; look at http://Powells.com – they publish customer reviews.
- Ask a librarian if your branch has a blog for patrons to post book reviews (Example: Seattle Library offers an on-line review form http://www.spl.org/default.asp?pageID=collection_readinglists_reviewform)
- Amazon.com
- Borders.com   Barnesandnoble.com   Booksamillion.com

Here's one of the reviews I wrote for Rita Lakin (a name I respect)
Teresa LeYung Ryan http://WritingCoachTeresa.com
Rating: ★★★★★ 5 stars
Review Title: Friendship Adventure Romance---the Whole Schmeer
I liked the first four novels in the Gladdy Gold series by Rita Lakin. This fifth adventure, *Getting Old Is a Disaster*, is even more exciting. You have to read it. Ms. Lakin is a smooth mystery writer--main plot and subplots so beautifully blended into a satisfying read. Sobering subject matters (Alzheimer's toll; Holocaust survivor's nightmares) plus crime-solving and friendship and romance, and even goofiness. Like being with a good friend, I didn't want the story to end. Oh, but what an ending!
Tags: *adventure, Alzheimer's, friendship, fun, gladdy gold, heroine, mental illness, holocaust, humor florida, mystery, rita lakin, romance, sleuths*

Day 11 YOUR TURN Today's Date: _____

Write the name of an author YOU admire and respect and the book title written by this author (a book that you've read)

_____

Compose a short review:

Tags:

Secret Key #5 into the lock
Remember:
Publish your reviews on your own website/blog and also on **websites of booksellers, the authors' or their publishers', and libraries (where** *your* **future fans now go to look for books similar to yours). Always give your full name, your website or blog address, and, your mission statement. If you have a published book, add the words**: author of _____ (your book title) **after your name.**

Save reviews you've written into a file so that you can use it again and again on other sites. **I say** write something once but publish it in multiple places.

☐   **check box after you've submitted the review to a bookseller's site.**

☐   **check box after you've submitted the review to a library's site.**

☐   **check box after you have published the review on your website/blog.**

☐   **check box after you have submitted the review on the author's site or the publisher's site (or you have emailed the author or publisher or author's agent).**

☐   **Where else?**

_____

Day 12   REACH OUT, *NOT* STRESS OUT

Remember what I said yesterday about **writing something once** but **publishing it in multiple places**?

If you're lucky enough to live in an area that offers a local newspaper, take a look at that paper. There must be at least one article or editorial comment that relates to a subject matter that you write about or a topic that is occupying your thoughts this week. Maybe you get your news on-line. Look at the headlines and choose an article to read.

A Letter-to-the-Editor is a powerful way to present your point of view on a community concern. Even if your letter (via email) doesn't get published by the local newspaper (in print or on-line), you can publish it on your website/blog, and, you can submit the letter to regional and national newspapers. **Local concerns usually echo across the country; national concerns touch all localities.**

EXAMPLE: When I found out that the city I live in was going to slash library hours at six branches, I needed to use my writer's voice to speak up. The following piece took me only 5 minutes to write. The keywords ("tags") had come from a flyer that another library advocate had emailed me. I copied and pasted text, **added my hook "Who needs our mighty voices?"** and **enhanced the bullet points**. That simple! I emailed it to the editor of my local newspaper and it got published because the piece **offered information and resources**. **The subject line I used:** Letter to Editor Re: Kids, Seniors, Job-Seekers / Libraries / Oakland Proposed Budget

---

Dear Editor:
Who needs our mighty voices? Library patrons of Oakland, CA.
- Kids who go to these safe places to read and do homework
- Seniors who make communities solid
- Unemployed adults using resources and the Internet for job-search

Bring family and friends and attend the Public Meetings regarding the city budget and tell Council Members directly. At the City Council Chambers at Oakland City Hall, 1 Frank H Ogawa Plaza.

Next Public Meeting: (I included date, time and link to City Hall's webpage)
Call or email the mayor and council and tell them how you feel about keeping all library branches open all week.   (I included the list of names, phone numbers and email addresses)
OTHER WAYS TO HELP? Tell friends, coworkers & neighbors about
http://savethelibraries.spaces.live.com
Sincerely,
Teresa LeYung Ryan , Oakland resident and author, Advocate for Public Libraries
http://WritingCoachTeresa.com

Day 12 Today's Date: _____

REACH OUT, NOT STRESS OUT

YOUR TURN – reading

1. **What is your local newspaper?** _____

   Do you read it on-line? _____

2. **No local newspaper? Go to your favorite publication (in print or on-line) for news.**

   _____

3. **Look at headlines. Which one grabs you?**

   _____

4. **Read the story. List the keywords (subject matter/what; who; where; when; resources):**

   _____

   _____

   _____

   _____

   _____

   _____

   _____

   _____

   _____

Day 13   Today's Date: _____

REACH OUT, NOT STRESS OUT

YOUR TURN – determine word-count; compose

Look at the Letters-to-Editors that do get published. What's the maximum word-count? _____

Compose your Letter-to-Editor (Remember to offer information or resources or both; be concise.) Use keywords (tags) from the article you read as well as tags that you have identified for yourself in the preceding pages of this workbook.

To save time on typing lists (i.e. you're providing a list of names, phone numbers, etc.), find a website that would have that information, then, copy and paste data into your piece.

What's your hook? _____

First draft of your Letter-to-Editor:

Day 13 Today's Date: _____
REACH OUT, NOT STRESS OUT

YOUR TURN – polish and submit your composition

1. What is the newspaper's website? _____

2. Look for "Contact Us" on their website and find names and email addresses to submit "opinion" or "letter to editor"

_____

Tips:
Email the piece to yourself before emailing the editor.
- What does the email look like when you open it as the receiver?
- Did you remember to add a subject line?
- Did you do spellcheck?
- Is your message concise?
- Is the email a huge block of text that would overwhelm the editor?
- Did you include your full name, your title and contact information?
- Did you include your mission statement in the body of your letter?

3. Email the editor and CC or BCC yourself. Also, if you're emailing more than one newspaper, keep a record of when, who, and what you emailed.

Tips:

Do <u>not</u> call or email the editor to ask: "Have you received my letter/email to the editor/email?" Most newspapers also publish on-line. A few days after you emailed your letter, you can Google your own name and a couple of keywords in your piece to see if they did publish your letter. Or, if the newspaper's website has a search feature, then key in your name. It's exciting to see one's own name linked to an established publication. You might get a phone call from a friend or neighbor saying: "Hey, I read your letter to the editor. Good job."

Day 14 Today's Date: _____

REACH OUT, NOT STRESS OUT

YOUR TURN – use the same piece again and again and again

- **Publish your piece** (whether or not the newspaper publishes it) on your website/blog.

- **Keep names and contact information** in your email address book for future use; **Bookmark** website addresses on your computer.

- **Submit the same piece** to a regional and/or national newspaper. Or do the reverse—if your letter went to a national paper, email it to regional and local.

What is another newspaper's website? _____

Look for "Contact Us" on their website and find names and email addresses to submit "opinion" or "letter to editor"

REACH OUT SOME MORE

EXAMPLE:

I'm going to take advantage of the piece I wrote yesterday; let's see where else I can send it to.

Step 1: I look at my "tags" (keywords):
Advocate, author, budget, California, city hall, communities, council members, family, friends, homework, Internet, job seekers, kids, library, mighty voices, Oakland, Oakland City Council, public libraries, public meeting, read, safe place, save the libraries, resources, seniors, Teresa LeYung Ryan, unemployed

Step 2: I go to Google.com and type a variation or a combination of my "tags" in the search box to see if anyone else is using the same combination.

library advocacy

Day 14

Step 3: I press Google Search and look at the first page of results.

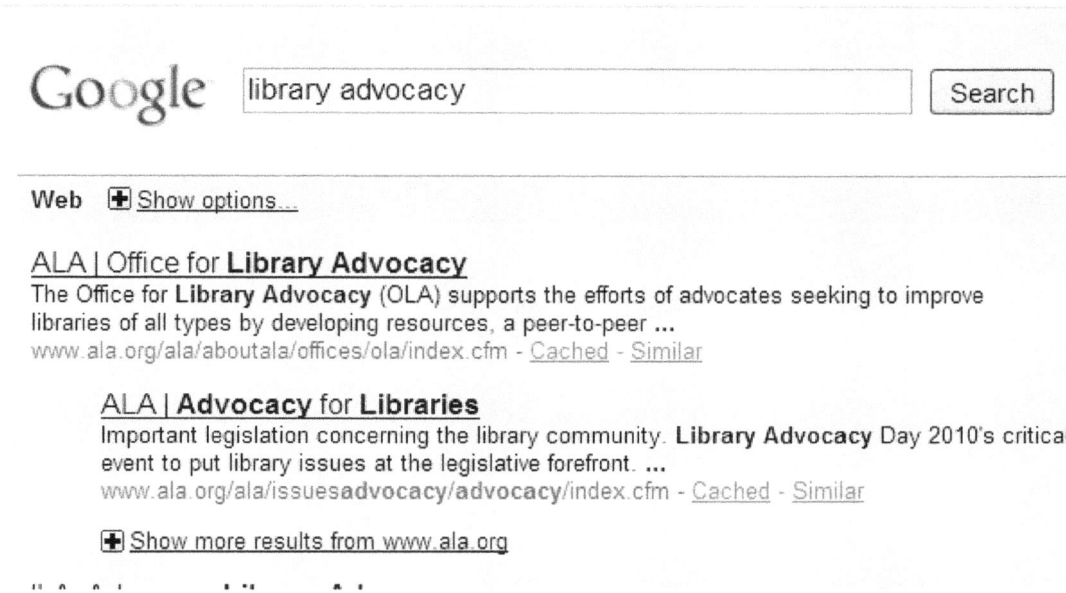

Google   library advocacy   [Search]

Web   ⊞ Show options...

ALA | Office for **Library Advocacy**
The Office for **Library Advocacy** (OLA) supports the efforts of advocates seeking to improve libraries of all types by developing resources, a peer-to-peer ...
www.ala.org/ala/aboutala/offices/ola/index.cfm - Cached - Similar

 ALA | **Advocacy** for **Libraries**
 Important legislation concerning the library community. **Library Advocacy** Day 2010's critical event to put library issues at the legislative forefront. ...
 www.ala.org/ala/issues**advocacy**/**advocacy**/index.cfm - Cached - Similar

 ⊞ Show more results from www.ala.org

The first result intrigues me because I recognize ALA (American Library Association). I click on the link:

ALA | Office for *Library Advocacy*

The Office for *Library Advocacy* (OLA) supports the efforts of advocates seeking to improve libraries of all types by developing resources, a peer-to-peer ... *www.ala.org/ala/aboutala/offices/ola/index.cfm*

Step 4: Now I'm at:
http://www.ala.org/ala/aboutala/offices/ola/index.cfm

Step 5: Scanning the left column, I see: **Office for Literacy & Outreach (OLOS)** That's interesting, so, I click on it. (see next visual)

Day 14

Home ▸ About ALA ▸ Offices ▸ Office for Library Advocacy (OLA)

About ALA

> Mission & History

> ALA & LIS Acronyms

> ALA Governing & Strategic Documents

˅ Offices

> Chapter Relations Office (CRO)

> Conference Services

> Development

> Governance

> Human Resources

> Information Technology & Telecommunication Services

> International Relations Office (IRO)

> Finance and Accounting

> Library

> Member & Customer Service

> Membership

> Office for Accreditation

> Office for Diversity

> Office for Human Resource Development and Recruitment (HRDR)

> Office for Information Technology Policy (OITP)

> Office for Intellectual Freedom (OIF)

˅ Office for Library Advocacy (OLA)

> Office for Literacy & Outreach (OLOS)

Office for Library Advocacy

ALA Office for Library Advocacy

American Library Association
50 East Huron Street
Chicago, Illinois 60611-2795
Phone: 312.280.2428
Fax: 312.280.3255
Email: ola@ala.org

Mission

The Office for Library Advocacy (OLA) supports the efforts of advocates seel
improve libraries of all types by developing resources, a peer-to-peer advoc
network, and training for advocates at the local, state and national level. In c
achieve this goal, OLA works closely with the Public Information Office, the
Relations Office, the Office for Government Relations, and other ALA units ii
advocacy on behalf of particular types of libraries or particular issues, in or
better integrate these efforts into the overall advocacy planning and strateg
association. OLA also works to cultivate future leadership in order to sustai
advocacy efforts of the association.

Oversight Groups

- ALA Committee on Library Advocacy (Standing, Council)
- Advocacy Training Subcommittee
- Advocacy Coordinating Group

Information on Office for Library Advocacy oversight groups

Events

Advocacy Institute

Popular Resources

Advocacy & Legislation
I Love Libraries

Step 6: Wow, on this page, I see: Visit our Outreach Columns blog **for stories from members! I know that most blogs provide opportunities for public comments (this is exactly what I want).**

Day 14

I click on <u>Outreach Columns blog</u>.

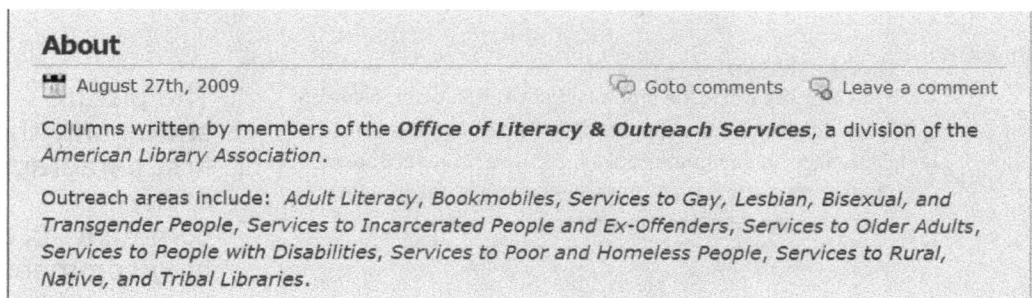

About

August 27th, 2009   Goto comments   Leave a comment

Columns written by members of the **Office of Literacy & Outreach Services**, a division of the American Library Association.

Outreach areas include: *Adult Literacy, Bookmobiles, Services to Gay, Lesbian, Bisexual, and Transgender People, Services to Incarcerated People and Ex-Offenders, Services to Older Adults, Services to People with Disabilities, Services to Poor and Homeless People, Services to Rural, Native, and Tribal Libraries.*

It's a blog with these categories:

- Adult Literacy
- Bookmobiles
- Services to Incarcerated People and Ex-Offenders
- Services to Older Adults

Step 7: I click on <u>Bookmobiles</u> I'm showing you the post I saw that day:

Search Results for: <u>library advocacy</u>

Bookmobiles and the ALA

By <u>admin</u> – September 1, 2009

By Michael Swendrowski, President – Specialty Vehicle Services, LLC., Chairman – ALA Subcommittee on Bookmobiles

Step 8: I click on this post and read . . .

The post written by Michael Swendrowski includes this statement: **The Subcommittee submitted a proposal and was approved by the ALA Public Awareness Committee to designate Wednesday of National Library Week as National Bookmobile Day, starting on Wednesday, April 14, 2010.**
[Coach Teresa here... this post grabs me. We, the residents of Oakland, have lost our Bookmobile due to City budget cuts.]

Step 9: I scroll down the computer screen until I see the boxes for comments.

Day 14

I chose to respond to Mr. Swendroswki's post on the Office for Literacy & Outreach Services (OLOS) blog about creating National Bookmobile Day.

'ost a comment

> Mr. Swendroswki,
> Your post regarding the proposal from ALA Subcommittee on Bookmobiles and the approval from ALA Public Awareness Committee to designate April 14, 2010 as National Bookmobile Day brings me joy. I will share this news with fellow authors and "Save the Libraries" advocates.

Some HTML is OK

Name   Teresa LeYung Ryan   (required)

Email   WritingCoachTeresa@gma   (required, but never shared)

Web   http://www.WritingCoachTe

[Post comment]   or, reply to this post via trackback

The picture shows only the first paragraph of my comment; in a blog comment box, you'd be able to scroll down and read the rest of your comment.

The box below shows you exactly what was inside the box.

- See how I used a salutation and a closing statement?
- **Words in bold font** = to show you the keywords (tags) I repeated from Mr. Swendroswki's blog post
- See how I gave a resource by referring to Save the Libraries in addition to drawing attention to the plight of Oakland Library Bookmobile?
- See my tailored signature block for this particular comment?

Mr. Swendroswki,

   Your post regarding the proposal from **ALA Subcommittee on Bookmobiles** and the approval from **ALA Public Awareness Committee** to designate **April 14, 2010** as **National Bookmobile Day** brings me joy. I will share this news with fellow authors and "Save the Libraries" advocates.

   In Oakland, CA, we have lost our bookmobile (and other library resources) when City officials passed the budget last year 2009. I invite all Bookmobile lovers/patrons to help by sharing their opinions on http://savethelibraries.spaces.live.com. Please click on" YOUR Bookmobile Story" and share yours. Or email your story to save-the-libraries@live.com.

   Thank you, ALA Subcommittee on Bookmobiles and ALA Public Awareness Committee! I will **celebrate** all Bookmobiles during **National Library Week 2010**.

Sincerely,
Teresa LeYung Ryan "Let's use our mighty voices to speak for libraries!"
Library Advocate, author, writing-career coach
http://WritingCoachTeresa.com

My repertoire grows and grows !

Day 15 Today's Date: _____

REACH OUT SOME MORE

You're going to take advantage of the piece you wrote the other day; let's see where else you can send it to.

Step 1: Look at your hook (lead):

_____

Step 2: Look at your "tags" (keywords & key phrases):

_____

_____

Step 3: Go to Google.com and type a combination of your "tags" in the search box to see if anyone else is using the same combination.

[   ]

Step 4: Press Google Search and look at the first page of results.

Anything interesting? List results here:

_____

_____

_____

Key in a combination of your tags plus the word **blog** in the Google search box. **List results here:**

_____

_____

Day 15   Today's Date: _____

You've found an article/video/interview/blog post that you'd want to comment on. Compose your comment or questions here:

Before you submit your comment/questions, **review this checklist. Once you press that [send] or [submit] button, there's no retrieving or revising it** (unless the recipient is someone who might let you get a second chance). Practice on my blogs; if you make a mistake, let me know and I'll delete your comment and you can submit a new one.

☐ Your piece contains the same keywords (tags) as those in the piece you're responding to.

☐ You include a salutation and a closing.

☐ You show your full name and website/blog address, so the readers will see your identification twice (not just once in the "From" line). We want readers to see our names connected to the issues/subject matters, again and again and again.

See you tomorrow!

Day 16   Today's Date: _____
REACH OUT/Double Back

▪ I'm going to add a few words to the comment I submitted yesterday and post on my own website/blog. I'll add a title, a photo or image (I'll go to Google Images and key in Oakland Bookmobile). I'll add the link to the Office for Literacy & Outreach Services (OLOS) blog (to cross reference) as well as links to library associations on the national and state level.   (This is what visitors to my blog will see.)

Writing Coach Teresa's Blog
Teresa helps writers build their names, beat the game, and be happily published

Let's Use Our Mighty Voices for Bookmobiles

Let's Bring Back Oakland Bookmobile

While rewriting the section in my new guide, the section on how to use words (tags) to find information on the World Wide Web, and, using "library advocacy" as an example, I came upon this...

search this site

Pages

Archives

Categories

Blogroll

Meta

I'll key in the "tags" for my post. (this is what visitors to my blog will see)

Tags: Teresa LeYung Ryan, 2010, Writing coach, writing career coach, Mighty Voices, Bookmobiles, ALA Subcommittee on Bookmobiles, ALA Public Awareness Committee, April 14, National Library Week, Oakland Public Library, American Library Association, California Library Association, kids, seniors, authors, Save the Libraries, Michael Swendrowski, Oakland Bookmobile, Oakland Library Bookmobile
Posted in writing coach / writing-career coach / manuscript

Day 16   Today's Date _____

YOUR TURN   REACH OUT/Double Back

☐ You're going to add a few words to the comment you submitted yesterday and post on your own website/blog.

☐ You'll add a title and you'll repeat title words in the post.

☐ You'll add a photo or image use (one that relates to the subject matter of your post). If you don't already have one on your computer, you can go to Google Images to find one; you don't have to insert a photo/image (don't spend too much time on finding one).

☐ You'll add the link to the webpage or blog post of the source that compelled you to submit your response yesterday (to cross reference) as well as other links that might be helpful to the readers (offering more resources).

☐ You'll key in the tags for your post. **Do invest time in keying in tags—** this is how people will find you—through tags (the words they key in when they're looking for something on the World Wide Web).

What will be the title for your post? What's the hook?

| |
| |

What photo or image would you like to insert?

| |
| |

What are the links/resources you'll offer?

| |
| |

What are the tags?

| |
| |

You're accomplishing so much! See you tomorrow !

Day 17   Today's Date: _____

You've accomplished <u>so</u> <u>much</u> in the past 16 days. I cheer for you!

Today, let's take another look at the PRESTIGIOUS PLACES that our celebrities have been invited to.

Coach Teresa's Example:

I Google "Maxine Hong Kingston" again. This result (Maxine interviewed by Bill Moyers) hooks my attention. How I'd love to be the guest of a feature interview on PBS someday.

Bill Moyers Journal . **MAXINE HONG KINGSTON** | PBS
May 25, 2007 ... On Memorial Day weekend, the JOURNAL presents an illuminatin
interview with **Maxine Hong Kingston**, acclaimed author of many books includi
www.pbs.org/moyers/journal/05252007/profile.html - Cached - Similar

YOUR TURN

Google one of your favorite celebrities again. Is there a result that hooks your attention? Any wishes?

Day 17

Coach Teresa's Example:

http://www.pbs.org/moyers/journal/05252007/profile.html

I go to the webpage (PBS/Bill Moyers JOURNAL) which has the transcript and the video (with a section for viewers' and readers' comments) of the May 25, 2007 Memorial Day weekend interview with Maxine. The description of the program is: [Bill Moyers sits down with Chinese-American author Maxine Hong Kingston to discuss her latest book *Veterans Of War, Veterans Of Peace*. For the past 15 years, Kingston has been working with veterans — more than 500 soldiers from World War II, from Vietnam, and now, from Iraq — as well as other survivors of war to convert the horrors they experienced into the words and stories that Kingston believes will help them cope and survive.]

I click on [Watch the video].   I want to see and hear Maxine. Wow! I write down what I remember from the video. Also, I read parts of the transcript.

> **My notes:**
> 30 years later, 35 years later, 39 years after coming home from the war. Secret. Don't burden my children, wife, husband. Forget it ever happened. Maxine reads excerpts written by the veterans and other survivors of war. Body escort, this soldier's job, to escort the body home. Post traumatic syndrome. The young pregnant wife opens the door for the two soldiers who have been assigned to say to her "...*regret to inform you that your* ..." When we meet to write, we don't talk. We take a vow of silence. We write. Maxine talks with her hands, her voice calm and reassuring.

Tomorrow I'll compose and submit my comment to the Bill Moyers JOURNAL Blog.

Day 17   Today's Date _____

YOUR TURN

What website/page (relating to your favorite celebrity) hooked your attention?

_____

Does that webpage take you to an even more interesting page?

Study the page. Read transcripts. Watch the video if there is one. Jot down the "tags" you read/heard:

I would like to hear from you. Go to my main website/blog http://writingcoachTeresa.com . Wherever this URL takes you, click on the **[TERESA'S BLOG]** tab. Then in my blog's search box, key in these words inside quotation marks: **"Day 17 of 22"**   **What sites hooked your attention? Tell me about them.**

Good work!   See you tomorrow!

Day 18   Today's Date: _____

If you need more time to read transcripts, articles, or watch the video from yesterday's assignment, then use today's time to do that. Or, if your research took you to another compelling site and you want to devote today's minutes to that, please go ahead.

Continue jotting down, names, keywords **and** phrases **(all tags) here:**

If you're ready to compose your comment/reaction, please go ahead.

Coach Teresa's Example:

Thank you, Mr. Bill Moyers, and everyone at The Journal and PBS for interviewing Ms. Maxine Hong Kingston on May 25, 2007 and making the transcript and video available on that site. Thanks for reading excerpts from Veterans of War, Veterans of Peace with Maxine. Each story/poem written by the veteran or loved one of a veteran carried much compassion. The book--what a magnificent gift from Maxine and the courageous men and women who transformed their suffering into what I call "word energy."

The interview and the excerpts got me thinking about my mom who was an orphan in China during WWII. She never talked about her experiences; at times a word would slip out, but, she would stop herself. She died in 2000 and I would like to believe that she's watching over me, encouraging me to write for people who cannot speak for themselves.

Maxine had inspired me to write my first book when in 1990 I read Woman Warrior: Memoirs of a Girlhood Among Ghosts. http://www.redroom.com/author/maxine-hong-kingston has other videos on Maxine and her work. Thanks again for the May 25, 2007 program.

Sincerely,

Teresa LeYung Ryan, author

I encourage adult-children of mentally-ill parents to speak openly about the stigmas their parents suffer.   http://LoveMadeOfHeart.com

POST A COMMENT

THE MOYERS BLOG is our forum for viewe
debating ideas and issues raised on BILL M
you to share your thoughts. We are comm
to preserve a civil, respectful dialogue, ou
any comments that we find unacceptable,
click here.

Name:

Email Address:

URL:

☐ Remember personal info?

Comments: (you may use HTML tags for s

Day 18   Today's Date _____

YOUR TURN
What are you going to comment on?

After you submit your comment or send your email, post the piece on your own blog.
Coach Teresa's Example:
On my blog, I'd add the link to The Moyers Journal/PBS site
http://www.pbs.org/moyers/journal/05252007/profile.html **and in the Tag box, I'd add these words/phrases:** Bill Moyers, The Journal, PBS, Maxine Hong Kingston, May 25, 2007, Veterans of War, Veterans of Peace, stories, poems, veterans, loved ones of veterans, compassion, courageous men and women, *Woman Warrior: Memoirs of a Girlhood Among Ghosts*, Red Room Authors, Teresa LeYung Ryan, *Love Made of Heart,* transform suffering into word energy, my mom, orphan in China, WWII, who cannot speak for themselves, word energy.

Then on the Red Room Authors website, I'll go to Maxine's blog and post a comment there. I too have a blog on Red Room Authors, so, I'll post there.

One piece is now published in 4 sites!

YOUR TURN. Where else could you send your piece?

You're getting good at this!   See you tomorrow!

Day 19   Today's Date _____

Wow! It's already Day 19. Only 3 more days to go to the finishing line! Only 3 more days to accepting your award.

Go to Google.com In the search box, key in the tags: **Chase Calendar of Events.**   If you see a link to McGraw Hill (MHProfessional), click on it. http://www.mhprofessional.com/?page=/mhp/categories/chases/content/special_months.html

I want you to see the list of special months (There are hundreds of them. i.e. Library Lovers' Month; National Black History Month; National Women's History Month; Gay & Lesbian Pride Month; National Make a Difference to Children Month; National Depression Education and Awareness Month; National Alzheimer's Disease Month; Asian/Pacific American Heritage Month). These special months give you more opportunities to put the spotlight on the themes/subject matters/issues you write about.

Of course there are the major holi<u>days</u> (Labor Day; Veterans Day; 4th of July; Mother's Day; Father's Day) that you could write about and link the holiday to the subject matter/issues/themes in your book. **The beauty of linking your name to a date that is celebrated or recognized for the entire month is that you'll have a whole month to re-use one piece of writing.**

After you find the webpage to the list of these designated special dates, focus on the special dates for the current month and next month.

As an example, I'll show the month of May here. I'll put an ← next to each cause that relates to a theme that I write about. The characters in my novel *Love Made of Heart* relate to these themes.

May

- Allergy/Asthma Awareness Month, Natl
- Arthritis Month, Natl
- Asian/Pacific American Heritage Month ← **my protagonist is Chinese American**
- Awareness of Medical Orphans Month
- Barbecue Month, Natl
- Better Hearing and Speech Month
- Bike Month, Natl
- Business Image Improvement Month, Intl
- Civility Month, Intl
- Creative Beginnings Month
- Ecodriving Month
- Egg Month, Natl
- Family Wellness Month ← **my protagonist did not have family wellness**
- Fibromyalgia Education and Awareness Month
- Freedom Shrine Month
- Get Caught Reading Month
- Gifts From the Garden Month
- Good Car-Keeping Month, Natl
- Haitian Heritage Month
- Hamburger Month, Natl
- Heal the Children Month ← **my protagonist was a broken child**
- Healthy Vision Month
- Hepatitis Awareness Month, Natl
- Huntington's Disease Awareness Month
- Internal Audit Awareness Month, Intl
- Jewish American Heritage Month ← **an ally for my protagonist is Jewish American**
- Latino Books Month
- Meditation Month, Natl
- Melanoma/Skin Cancer Detection and Prevention Month

- Mental Health Month, Natl ← **my protagonist's mother suffers from mental illness**
- Military Appreciation Month, Natl
- Motorcycle Safety Month
- Moving Month, Natl
- Older Americans Month
- Osteoporosis Awareness and Prevention Month, Natl
- Personal History Month ← **my protagonist has secrets in her personal history**
- Photo Month, Natl
- Physical Fitness and Sports Month, Natl
- Preservation Month, Natl
- REACT Month
- Revise Your Work Schedule Month
- Salad Month, Natl
- Salsa Month, Natl
- Smile Month, Natl
- Strike Out Strokes Month
- Stroke Awareness Month, Natl
- Sweet Vidalia Onion Month, Natl
- Teen CEO Month
- Teen Self-Esteem Month ← **my protagonist had no self-esteem as a teen**
- Tennis Month
- Ultraviolet Awareness Month
- Victorious Woman Month, Intl
- Vinegar Month, Natl
- Women's Health Care Month
- Young Achievers/Leaders of Tomorrow Month

Day 19

I choose National Mental Health Month. So, I key in those words in Google search; Google automatically adds the current year 2010 while I'm typing. Aren't they helpful!

I press Google Search button and up comes a list of sites. The first few don't interest me; the links look like they could be drug companies.

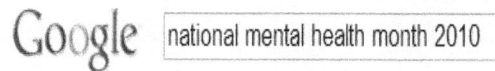

Google   national mental health month 2010

Aah, the next result does interest me. On Day 6, I had identified that "mental illness" is a subject matter I write about. Then on Day 9 I had found NAMI while looking for organizations whose mission statements reflect what I write about.

NAMI: *National* Alliance on *Mental* Illness | Multicultural Action ...

2010 Downloads (coming soon) will include: *National* Minority *Mental Health* Awareness *Month*   www.nami.org/minority**mentalhealthmonth**

This time, I'll do more than borrowing words from their mission statement. I click on "How You Can Help" and get links to:

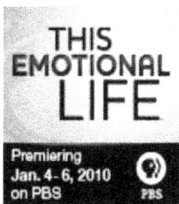

THIS EMOTIONAL LIFE
Premiering
Jan. 4- 6, 2010
on PBS

MINDS on the EDGE
If We Can Talk About
Mental Illness,

Contact Your Representatives

It is important that you **contact your state and national representatives** to ensure they are working for people with mental illness.

A list of current legislation impacting mental health is available along with an easy way to contact your representative with just a few clicks of a mouse.

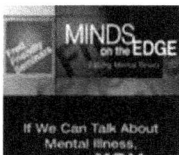

Fight Stigma

Often times the media portrays people with mental illness in an untruthful, unflattering, and hurtful light. You have the ability to set the record straight.

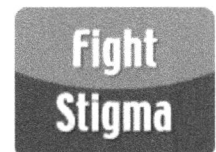

Contact Legislators

Fight Stigma

Day 19   Today's Date _____

YOUR TURN

You're at the Chase Calendar of Events?

What month and which special dates are you looking at?

_____

You Google the name of that special date. You could add the year or the name of the nearest metropolitan in the search box.

Anything interesting? Do you see any organization(s) from the exercises from Day 8 and Day 9 (when you were composing your mission statement)?

_____

_____

_____

_____

_____

_____

_____

See you tomorrow!

Day 20

Yesterday I researched; today I write/take action:

- I could write a short post on my blog about NAMI (give the organization's full name, its URL, its mission statement, and talk about my mission statement too).

- I could email my state and national representatives; I'll be sure to give my full name, my mission statement, and website or blog address.

- I could go to the article that **Ms. Glenn Close** (Emmy, Golden Globe and Tony Award winning actress) had written for **The Huffington Post** (I had found it on Day 9), and submit my comment, offer a resource from NAMI, and sign the comment with my name, mission statement and URL.

- Whatever I choose to do, I'll put a copy of it on my own blog and take time to list the "tags."

I choose writing to Ms. Close via the blog comment box on

http://www.huffingtonpost.com/glenn-close/mental-illness-the-stigma_b_328591.html

I see that I have to start an account in order to submit a comment to their blog. I'll do it. I am THE expert of my experiences; I want to thank Ms. Close for being candid; I want my name and mission statement linked to her messages in *The Huffington Post*.

HuffPost Social News

Already have an account?

Enter your HuffPost username and password

ENTER USERNAME

ENTER PASSWORD

Sign in

Forgot your Username or Password?

Sign up now!

f **Connect with Facebook**

Sign in with Twitter

YAHOO!

Join this site
Google Friend Connect

Day 20   Today's Date _____

Where did yesterday take you?

_____

Which organization/media are you reaching out to?

_____

Which Blogs?

_____

Will you be attending events sponsored by organizations that share your mission statements?

_____

Find out if and when they would need a speaker and follow through.

_____

Brainstorm/Compose here or start a list of contact names & info.

_____

Are you excited about your name and where your name is going? Google YOUR own name inside quotation marks again.

Day 21
WHO AM I TODAY?   Coach Teresa's Examples:

My name is:	Teresa LeYung Ryan
Tags synonymous with <u>what</u> I write about:	**stigmas; immigrant experiences; mental illness in family; self-forgiveness; violence at home; voice in writing**
Tags synonymous with <u>who</u> I write for:	**Chinese-American women; courageous immigrant women; mentally-ill parents; survivors of violence**
My Name is THE search result <u>when particular tags target</u> me: "Who I Can Help" + "How I Can Help"	**Target Mission Statements** • Teresa LeYung Ryan **sheds light** on stigmas suffered by immigrant women, men, and children in the U.S.A. • Teresa LeYung Ryan **speaks out** on behalf of mentally-ill parents who suffer secret agonies. • Teresa LeYung Ryan **inspires** survivors of violence to find their voices through writing.
My messages are in alignment with:	Maxine Hong Kingston's http://redroom.com/author/maxine-hong-kingston Glenn Close's http://www.bringchange2mind.org/ National Alliance on Mental Illness's http://nami.org/ Stamp Out Stigma's http://www.stampoutstigma.net Carmen Lee, founder) Family Violence Prevention Fund http://endabuse.org National Coalition Against Domestic Violence www.ncadv.org
I am the author of:	*Love Made of Heart*; essays; short stories; articles; speeches; my blog posts; *Build Your Writer's Platform & Fanbase in 22 Days*

Day 21   Today's Date _____

Tomorrow is Graduation/Finishing Line. Can you believe it? Let's take a fresh look at WHO YOU ARE on Day 21.

My name is:	
Tags synonymous with **what** I write about:	
Tags synonymous with **who** I write for:	
My Name is THE search result <u>when particular tags *target* me</u>: "*Who* I Can Help" + "*How* I Can Help"	
My messages are in alignment with:	
I am the author of:	

No peeking.

Tomorrow is YOUR Big Day.

Turn the page tomorrow.

Day 22   Today's Date _____

Dear Writer,

As I write this page, my heart feels light and joy for you.

When you "stick to" a program for 21 days, you develop a new habit. If the new habit is to continue building your name with your words, then it's a wonderful habit. I celebrate YOU!

Today, Day 22, is for bragging about and honoring the New You. Go to http://WritingCoachTeresa.com and click on [TERESA'S BLOG]

In the blog search box, key in "Build MY Platform Hall of Fame" then press the enter key. Click on the title:

"Build MY Platform Hall of Fame"

Write your acceptance speech by:

- introducing yourself with your newest mission statement.
- giving us a glimpse into your hopes and dreams for your illustrious writing career.

   If you cannot access the Internet today, compose your acceptance speech here and publish it on my blog and yours later.

Your Acceptance Speech:

I'll see you! Your name. Again. And again. And again!

Post-Graduate Goodies. Coach Teresa here to demonstrate the power of keywords and key phrases ("tags") in your mission statement. Look what happens when someone (who don't already know my name or my book) uses a search engine and key in the tags: **speak openly about the stigmas suffered**

Look how the Internet found the webpages that contain those tags.

www.thewritespot.us is the website for Writers Forum of Petaluma. Marlene Cullen, the founder of this forum, had invited me and my pal Elisa Southard to give a talk. Marlene had posted my bio (which included my new mission statement which includes the words: speak openly about the stigmas suffered).

The 4th result on this page is the remarkable article by Glenn Close for *The Huffington Post*. Ms. Close had used the same phrases that I use.

The 5th and 8th results are ME! My blog; and my webpage for my novel *Love Made of Heart*.

Do you see how powerful "the right tags" are? More fans will find you when they're looking for a topic/issue/subject matter/theme AND they accidently come across your blog/website. This is the magic of name-building !

Google | speak openly about the stigmas suffered

Writers Forum - Marlene Cullen
... Made of Heart to inspire adult children of mentally-ill parents to speak openly stigmas their parents suffer. http://WritingCoachTeresa.com ...
www.thewritespot.us/gpage2.html - Cached - Similar -

Stigmas Surrounding Eating Disorders | Here to Help, A BC ...
My personal experience has to do with my mother who **suffered** from ... Today, person, she can **speak openly** about her medication and her support ...
www.heretohelp.bc.ca/stories/stigma-discrimination/exp/11 - Cached -

After suicide takes their loved ones, survivors find purpose - CNN.
After losing loved ones to suicide, some speak out in hopes of helping ... loss speak out about the experience despite the stigma attached. ... His maternal g suffered from the same disease but never shared his ...
www.cnn.com/2009/HEALTH/11/19/suicide.survivors.../index.html - Cached -

Glenn Close: Mental Illness: The **Stigma** of Silence
Oct 21, 2009 ... It is an odd paradox that a society, which can now speak openly figures **suffered** from mental illness including Florence Nightingale. ...
www.huffingtonpost.com/.../mental-illness-the-stigma_b_328591.html - Cache

Writing Coach Teresa's Blog
... first book Love Made of Heart to inspire adult-children of mentally-ill parents openly and unabashedly about the stigmas their parents suffer." ...
writingcoachteresa.wordpress.com/ - Cached -

Mental Health Overview
Some people believe that children do not suffer from mental illness. ... Talk op mental illness. Talking about your own mental illness or the ... Speak up when arises. If someone expresses a stigmatizing attitude, ...
www.netwellness.org/healthtopics/mentalhealth/overview.cfm - Cached - Simil

Coverage of Cho may renew **stigma** of mental illness, experts say
Aug 26, 2007 ... Those who **suffer** from selective mutism do not "refuse" to spe People in the region who were once willing to **speak openly** about ...
www.roanoke.com/vtinvestigation/wb/129491 - Cached - Similar -

Love Made of Heart - an immigrant daughter's journey to self ...
Love Made of Heart inspires adult-children of mentally-ill parents to speak ope unabashedly about the stigmas that their parents suffer. ...
www.lovemadeofheart.com/Love-Made-of-Heart-an-immigrant-daughter's-jour forgiveness.html - Cached -

Psychiatrists **suffer** from **stigma** too -- Persaud 24 (8): 284 ...
by R Persaud - 2000 - Cited by 11 - Related articles
Psychiatrists suffer from stigma too ... meant to represent — and who nomina

This page is for the new YOU. Go to a search engine (like Google.com). In the search box, type in a few keywords or a key phrase from your mission statement. Print the first few pages of search results. Take a close look at the lists.

Do you see how powerful it is to link "the right tags" to your name? Fans and more fans will find you when they're looking for a topic/subject matter/theme; they will come across your blog/website *accidently*. Or, is it *incidentally*! How thankful they will be. This is the magic of name-building !

You can attach the printouts to the inside of the back cover of this workbook.

Google YOUR own name inside quotation marks. How many search results do you see? _____ How about number of visitors to your website/blog/YouTube, etc.? _____ _____
Compare today's results to Day 2's results.

Do you want to know if your fans are talking about you on cyberspace? Go to Google.com Click on [more] then click on [even more]. Sign up for [Alerts]. Inside their [search terms] box, key in your name and/or your URL and/or your book title. Google Alerts will email you when someone "tags" you. Then it's up to you to reach out to your fans.

If you belong to a writers' club, please ask the program chair to visit my website. I love conducting "Major League Tryouts with Coach Teresa to Build Your Writer's Name."

If you need one-on-one consultation, contact me through my blog or go to my website and click on [Contact Coach Teresa].

Happy platform building!
Writing Career Coach Teresa

Form a study-group, split the cost, and hire Coach Teresa to:

- help you identify themes and archetypes, build your platform, and choose the right publishing route
- guide you in designing and growing your blog (to showcase your expertise and experiences)
- show you computer-navigating shortcuts and how to easily "find stuff" on the World Wide Web

Like my clients, you might have spent many months, perhaps years, writing and rewriting your project. And, you've decided to pursue either an agent (who earns his/her commission when he/she sells a client's work to a publishing house) or an acquisition editor (whose job is to buy authors' works for the publishing house he/she works for). Let's say you've done your homework and have compiled a list of agents or acquisition editors who specialize in the kind of project (commodity) you wish to sell.

An agent or acquisition editor receives hundreds of pitches/query letters each week. What can you do to catch these folks' attention? Use the right bait—your platform. Make every word count.

Whether you're pitching in person, over the phone, through an Email, or by old-fashion mail, keep this in mind—the pitch has three components:
- who needs your project—the target readers
- the unique qualities about your commodity
- why you are the perfect author for this work—because of your platform

Whether or not you are your own publisher, you can use part of your pitch as book jacket copy, press releases, and promotional material to attract readers and media attention.

Do you write prescriptive non-fiction, narrative non-fiction or fiction? _____
What's your specific genre? _____ See page 82.

Here are examples—How to Pitch:

* * * * * * * * * * * * * * *

Genre: (prescriptive non-fiction) *Self-Help/Metaphysical/Psychology*

Most people over the age of 10 dream at least four to six times per night.

Through *My Dreams: A Simple Guide to Dream Interpretation,* I can help everyone interpret dreams by combining their feelings with personal symbolism, dream what they want to dream, and improve their waking lives through their dreams.

I am Angie Choi, a certified hypnotherapist who has utilized radio, television, workshops, classes, articles, and a website to educate and inspire people to tap into their dreaming potential. I've worked with school districts, youth groups and community-based organizations. **http://alivehypnosis.com**

* * * * * * * * * * * * * *

Genre: (narrative non-fiction) Memoir

There are more than 38-million boom-generation women in this country. Through my book, I show middle-aged women how to cope with family and social pressures while dealing with their own mortality issues.

My memoir, **Oldham Street**, is about my journey from east coast to west bearing a secret pain, the long slow death of my father, the end of my counseling career and a ten-year relationship. I knocked on a lemon-colored door on a short block in San Francisco. In the next twelve years, the woman who opened that door, along with the other quirky characters in the neighborhood, inadvertently joined me in a process that brought me home to myself and into a comfortable role as the matriarch of my tribe.

I am Lynn Scott:

- **author** of *A Joyful Encounter: My Mother, My Alzheimer Clients, and Me* (a memoir about the abundance of spirit that I found among my Alzheimer clients).
- Contributor to eight anthologies of fiction, memoir, and poetry.
- a guest on OPRAH and other talk shows.

http://lynnscottbooks.com and **http://lynnscott.wordpress.com**

* * * * * * * * * * * * * *

Genre: (fiction) Women's Issues; Humor

39% of the 68 million women employed in the U.S. work in management, professional, and related occupations. Through my book **Katie Carlisle**, I show women how to hold onto their integrity, humor, and vision . . . in spite of having to fight sexism in the corporate world.

Katie Carlisle has been lucky enough to have a mentor (her boss) who has taken her to a point where her promotion is pretty well guaranteed. Only then everything goes wrong. Her beloved mentor leaves the company under a cloud; his successor is a man whom Katie hates and fears; and a downward spiral in her fortunes starts. This is the story of a smart woman's struggle to hold onto her integrity, humor and vision in spite of the tumult around her—and her eventual triumph.

I am Margaret Davis. I have a doctorate from Stanford University in Sociology, with a specialization in the structure and behavior of formal organizations. I have had two non-fiction books published in my field. **Katie Carlisle**, a humorous spoof on everyday life in a large corporation, is a work of fiction **I am also the author** of **Straight Down the Middle**, a family drama involving a young mother's efforts to do what is best for her child while trying to come to terms with her own sexuality. **http://margaretdavisbooks.com**

Articulating my mission statements—owning my platform and making my name stand for something—attracts targeted audience and connects me to people who have paved the way for me or are on similar paths or want to follow my career footsteps:

Teresa LeYung Ryan with **Maxine Hong Kingston & Jeanne Wakatsuki Houston** at 2005 **"Save Salinas Libraries/ Emergency Read-Out"** —photo by **Lyle Ryan**

Teresa LeYung Ryan finds out that *Love Made of Heart* has been added to the collection at the Daniel E. Koshland **San Francisco History Center**—photo by author **Elisa Southard**

Librarian **Patti Fashing** & teacher **Kathy Richman** invite **Teresa LeYung Ryan** back, to celebrate the 100th birthday of the **Salinas Public Libraries.**

Love Made of Heart is recommended by the **California School Library Association** and the **California Reading Association;** nominated for the **Asian American Literary Awards**—photo by author **Cheri Eplin**

As a community spirit, **Teresa LeYung Ryan** participates in **"Walk to End Poverty**—photo by peace activist & author **Lakshmi Hannah Kerner**

The Chinese word for 'love' is made up of many brush strokes. In the center of the word 'love' is the word 'heart.' Love is made of heart...

Love Made of Heart is in **public libraries** in the **United States, the United Kingdom, New Zealand, Australia,** and **Singapore.**

Love Made of Heart is at **Boston Public library, in a special collection** donated by **Women's National Book Association**

Teresa LeYung Ryan delivers keynote speech on **"Denim Day"** and **"Take Back the Night"** during **Sexual-Assault-Awareness-Month** for **Community Violence Solutions**.

Remember me as the author who says: YES! to compassion on mental illness, and NO! to domestic violence and child abuse!

Remember me as the author who honors all immigrant experiences (Pilgrams then and now, from all over the globe).

Remember me as the author who says: Advocate for public libraries and public schools to keep the USA a "literate nation."

Teresa LeYung Ryan reconnects with communit y at **Asian Heritage Street Celebration** (Thank you, author **Margie Yee Webb**!) with authors **Kiyo Sato** and **Frances Kakugawa** and **SF History Center** archivist Susan Goldstein.

Annie Yee recognized *Love Made of Heart* book cover **at Asian Heritage Street Celebration** and **reconnected with Teresa LeYung Ryan**

As a **writing career coach**, Teresa LeYung Ryan says: "Reach out, not stress out, when building your writer's name/platform." Teresa's advice for fiction and non-fiction authors: "To attract attention, talk about the issues and subject matters first, not the synopsis. Hook with your mission statement."

Teresa LeYung Ryan with **Barbara Santos** and **Elisa Southard**—presenting and having fun at the exciting **San Francisco Writers Conference**

Teresa LeYung Ryan with Women's National Book Association fellow-members **Amy Gorman, Kate Farrell, Rita Lakin, Pat Windom, Marcia Canton, Ph.D.** at **Sonoma County Book Festival** – photo by **Lyle Ryan** Teresa got to be a minor minor character in Rita's *Getting Old is a Disaster* (5th book in the Gladdy Gold mystery series)

Teresa LeYung Ryan as a **panelist** at the **Commonwealth Club** with **Scott James, a.k.a. Kemble Scott** & **Elisabeth Block**; moderator **Paula Hendricks**; producer **Kevin O'Malley** (photo by poet **Yolande Barial**). Teresa's and Kemble's first novels are published by Kensington Publishing Corp.

Teresa LeYung Ryan with **Carmen Lee**, founder of **Stamp Out Stigma** (on mental illness).

Pam Reitman greets **Teresa LeYung Ryan** at "Building a Caring Community for Mental Illness" symposium."

Teresa LeYung Ryan talks about domestic violence as "terrorism at home" with Sociology students at U.C. Berkeley – photo by Prof. Dan Haytin

Mission Statements

- Teresa LeYung Ryan **sheds light** on stigmas suffered by immigrant women, men, and children in the U.S.A.
- Teresa LeYung Ryan **speaks out** on behalf of mentally-ill parents who suffer secret agonies.
- Teresa LeYung Ryan **inspires** survivors of violence to find their voices through writing.

Flanked by authors **Elisa Southard** & **Mary E. Knippel**, **Teresa LeYung Ryan** as actress in **Eve Ensler's** *Vagina Monologues*; directed by **Kathryn McCarty** to benefit **Community Violence Solutions** (photo by **Ellen Gailing**)

Teresa LeYung Ryan, author of *Love Made of Heart*, speaks to **Advance Composition English-as-a-Second-Language students** (in **Victor Turks**'s, **Miriam Queen**'s and **Patricia Costello**'s classes at **City College of San Francisco**).

on television
on radio
in newsprint
on cyberspace
at book stores
at high schools, colleges, universities
at libraries
at writers conferences
at county fairs and
other community events

Here are some categories/genres used by booksellers:

- Anthologies
- Arts & Photography
- Autobiographies
- Biographies & Memoirs
- Business & Investing
- Children's Fiction
- Children's Non-Fiction
- Christian
- Comics & Graphic Novels
- Computers & Internet
- Cooking, Food & Wine
- Crafts & Hobbies
- Diet
- Drama
- Entertainment
- Erotica
- Fiction
- Gay & Lesbian
- Health, Mind & Body
- Historical Fiction
- History
- Home & Garden
- Horror
- Humor
- Literary Fiction
- Medical
- Metaphysical
- Mystery & Thrillers
- Nonfiction
- Outdoors & Nature
- Paranormal
- Parenting & Families

- Poetry
- Politics
- Professional & Technical
- Psychology
- Publishing
- Puzzles & Games
- Reference
- Religion
- Romance
- Romance Suspense/Thriller
- Science
- Science Fiction & Fantasy
- Self-Help
- Short Stories
- Social Science
- Spirituality
- Sports
- Teens
- Textbooks
- Travel
- True Crime
- Westerns
- Women's Fiction

Children's Books-Age Groups

- Babies & Toddlers
- Ages 4-8
- Ages 9-12

Add genres here: _____

_____

_____

Books I'm Reading
and
Books I'd Like to Read
(include genres that I haven't read before)

Websites I Bookmark
and
Visit on a Regular Basis

Events I'd Like to Attend this Year
and
People to Go With

Collecting Photos of Myself
In My Community

Coach Teresa says: "Rename photo files so that your name is part of the file name, not a bunch of numbers generated by your camera."

What Gives Me Joy?

Quotes from Me; Quotes from People I Respect
(a few of Coach Teresa's favorite quotes on page 100)

Bibliography
Books, Plays, TV Shows, Movies & Websites Referenced

A Joyful Encounter: My Mother, My Alzheimer Clients, and Me by Lynn Scott
Charlotte's Web by E.B. White
Getting Old Is A Disaster; Getting Old Is Tres Dangereux by Rita Lakin
Love Made of Heart by Teresa LeYung Ryan
My Dreams: A Simple Guide to Dream Interpretation by Angie Choi
Straight Down the Middle by Margaret Davis
Where the Heart Is by Billie Letts
Woman Warrior; Chinaman; Fifth Book of Peace; To Be a Poet by Maxine Hong Kingston
Wordsworth the Poet by Frances Kakugawa
Lost in Yonkers by Neil Simon

Dr. Kildare; Peyton Place; Mod Squad; Dynasty; The Rookies; Nightingales; Flamingo Road (television shows associated with Rita Lakin)

I'll be Seeing You; Primrose Path; Storm Warning; Twist of Fate; Kitty Foyle: The Natural History of a Woman (movies Ginger Rogers starred in)

22DaysToBuildPlatform.com   *Build Your Writer's Platform & Fanbase In 22 Days*

ala.org/ala/aboutala/offices/ola/index.cfm   American Library Association

Amazon.com

askmepc.com   askmepc-webdesign.com   wordpresscentral.org   Linda Lee, cyberspace guru

barbsantos.wordpress.com & **redroom.com/author/barbara-santos**   Barbara Santos, co-author of *Practice Aloha*; *Maui Onion Cookbook*; *Maui Tacos Cookbook*

Barnesandnoble.com   Barnes & Noble Booksellers

Bayside-indexing.com   Nancy Mulvany, indexer, author of *Indexing Books*

Blockbusterplots.com   Martha Alderson, international plot consultant, author of *Blockbuster Plots Pure & Simple*

Booksamillion.com   Books-A-Million

booktour.com

Borders.com   Borders Books & Music

breakthroughthenoise.com & **elisaonassignment.com**   Elisa Southard, travel writer, marketing coach, keynote speaker, author of *Break Through the Noise*; *Big City Travel Skills*

bringchange2mind.org   Glenn Close

BuildMyNameBeatTheGame.com   Teresa LeYung Ryan

calwriters.org   California Writers Club

CoaxingCreativity.com & **OpenUpToYourCreativity.com**   Mary E. Knippel, creativity mentor, author of *Creativity and Crisis*

dearjane.info   Rebecca Martin, employment & career consultant

DeborahGrossman.com   Deborah Grossman, poet laureate, author of *Goldie and Me*

dupagehealth.org/mental_health/stigma.html

dystel.com   Dystel & Goderich Literary Management; Stacey Glick is Teresa LeYung Ryan's agent for *Love Made of Heart*

ebparks.org   East Bay Regional Park District

en.wikipedia.org/wiki

endabuse.org   The Family Violence Prevention Fund

facebook.com

GailMdesign.com   Gail Cao Mazhari graphic and web designs

Goodreads.com

huffingtonpost.com/glenn-close/mental-illness-the-stigma_b_328591.html
Glenn Close's article

indiebound.org   independent book stores and booksellers

Judithmarshall.net   Judith Marshall, author of *Husbands May Come and Go but Friends are Forever*

kemblescott.com   Kemble Scott, pen name for fiction of Scott James-- columnist for *The Bay Citizen* whose stories appear each week in *The New York Times*

Kensingtonbooks.com   Kensington Publishing Corp. NY   and John Scognamiglio

larsen-pomada.com   Michael Larsen & Elizabeth Pomada, literary agents, authors

Librarything.com   LibraryThing connects you to people who read what you do.

LinkedIn.com   LinkedIn professional networking

linkedin.com/pub/lori-noack/15/ab/3a1 Lori Noack, editor, book designer

looktothestars.org/celebrity   Look to the Stars—the world of celebrity giving

LoveMadeOfHeart.com   Teresa LeYung Ryan, *Love Made of Heart*

LynnScottbooks.com   Lynn Scott, *A Joyful Encounter: My Mother, My Alzheimer Clients, and Me*

MarciaNaomiBerger.com ; marriagemaven.com ; marriagemeetings.com
Marcia Naomi Berger, author of *Marriage Meeting Starter Kit*

mayoclinic.com/health/mental-health/MH00076

mhprofessional.com/?page=/mhp/categories/chases/content/special_months.html
Chase's Calendar of Events

nami.org   National Alliance on Mental Illness

nami.org/minoritymentalhealthmonth

nami.org/template.cfm?Section...Stigma... -

ncadv.org   National Coalition Against Domestic Violence

pbs.org/moyers/journal/05252007/profile.html   Public Broadcasting Service—Bill Moyers Journal

Powells.com   Powell's Books

Redroom.com   Red Room—where the writers are

Redroom.com/author/maxine-hong-kingston   Maxine Hong Kingston

ritalakin.com   Rita Lakin, author of the Gladdy Gold comedy-mystery series

rp-author.com/Adams   Luisa Adams, author of *Woven of Water* (Robertson Publishing)

savethelibraries.spaces.live.com Save the Libraries Advocate Patrick Camacho

savingcinderella.ning.com   Ellen H. Taliaferro, MD, FACEP

sfwriters.org   San Francisco Writers Conference

spl.org/default.asp?pageID=collection_readinglists_reviewform   Seattle Public Library

stampoutstigma.net   Carmen Lee, founder of Stamp Out Stigma

stampoutstigma.net/famous.html-

TeresaLeYungRyan.com   Teresa LeYung Ryan, author, manuscript consultant, writing-career coach, publisher

thefreedictionary.com

thewritespot.us   Marlene Cullen's Writers Forum of Petaluma

twitter.com

usa.usembassy.de/society-demographics.htm

VickiWeiland.wordpress.com   Vicki Weiland, editor/book doctor

Wikipedia.org

wnba-books.org   and   **wnba-sfchapter.org**   Women's National Book Association

Wordpress.com   to get free blogs

WritingCoachTeresa.com   Teresa LeYung Ryan

WritingCoachTeresa.wordpress.com   Teresa LeYung Ryan's blog at wordpress.com

YolandeBarial.wordpress.com   Yolande Barial, poet, author, spoken word producer

Acknowledgments

Lori Noack for workbook layout and Martha Alderson for pure & simple plot (yes! workbooks.

Nancy Mulvany for indexing.

Judith Marshall, Michael Larsen, and Margaret Davis for reconfiguring the title of this workbook.

Gail Cao Mazhari for front and back cover design.

Cheri Eplin for back cover photo.

Fellow members in my mastermind group: Linda Lee, Mary E. Knippel, Rebecca Martin, Lori Noack, Martha Alderson, Luisa Adams.

Mary E. Knippel, Yolande Barial, Lynn Scott, and all the other wonderful writers who completed the exercises in *Build Your Name, Beat the Game*: *Be Happily Published*.

Elisa Southard for helping me understand that powerful tool which she calls the "talking tagline" in her book *Break Through the Noise: 9 Tools to Propel Your Marketing Message*

Fellow members in Fab Five: Vicki Weiland, Deborah Grossman, Elisa Southard, Barbara Santos.

California Writers Club, Women's National Book Association, & SF Writers Conference friends (A - Z).

Kind hearts in the literary community (including folks at libraries, schools, stores, online organizations, book industry; folks who orchestrate classes, workshops, conferences and festivals; folks who produce newsprint and online publications; folks who create radio, television, and online programs).

Stacey Glick at Dystel & Goderich Literary Management and John Scognamiglio at Kensington Publishing Corp. NY (my agent & editor, respectively, for my novel *Love Made of Heart*) for their insight as to the competitive nature of the publishing industry.

Christy Pinheiro & Nick Russell for writing *The Step-By-Step Guide to Self-Publishing for Profit!*

CreateSpace, for distribution of this workbook.

Michael Larsen, Jay Conrad Levinson & Rick Frishman for writing *Guerrilla Marketing for Writers*: *100 Weapons for Selling Your Work*.

Lynn Scott, Judith Marshall, Marcia Naomi Berger (former Critique Group) for their support in broadcasting my mission statements.

My East Bay Regional Park District network, writing colleagues, sweetheart, family, and personal friends (A through Z) who have encouraged me to write this workbook.

Rita, my Number One Angel.

Writers who are also my clients whom I cheer for, always.

How would you find the websites/blogs of the folks I'm acknowledging? In the bibliography. Also, you will find them and many others on my "Resources for Writers" page on http://WritingCoachTeresa.com and my facebook page.

Index

**BUILD YOUR WRITER'S PLATFORM & FANBASE IN 22 DAYS:
*Attract Agents, Editors, Publishers, Readers, and Media Attention NOW***

Quotes from Writing Career Coach Teresa LeYung Ryan:

"Build your name, beat the game. You too can be happily published"

"To write *is* my labor of love. To sell what I write *is* doing business."

"Reach out, not stress out."

"Make your name synonymous with the themes/issues/subject matters in your literary works."

"I write for people who cannot speak for themselves."

"A platform is not what I stand on, but what I stand for."

Look for other books, e-books, and resources
by
Teresa LeYung Ryan

Visit:

http://22DaysToBuild.com
http://WritingCoachTeresa.com
http://22DaysToBuildPlatform.com

www.ingramcontent.com/pod-product-compliance
Lightning Source LLC
Chambersburg PA
CBHW080208300326
41934CB00039B/3411